David Adam was born in Aln was Vicar of Danby on the Nort 20 years, where he discovered t in the Celtic pattern. His first book of these, *The Edge of Glory*, achieved immediate popularity. He has since published several collections of prayers and meditations based on the Celtic tradition and the lives of the Celtic saints. His books have been translated into several languages, including Finnish and German, and have appeared in American editions and also editions in India. Many of his prayers have now been set to music and are available on CDs. After 13 years as Vicar of Holy Island, where he had taken many retreats and regularly taught school groups on prayer, David moved to Waren Mill in Northumberland, from where he continues his work and writing.

# DAVID ADAM

# LOVE THE WORLD

First published in Great Britain in 2018

Society for Promoting Christian Knowledge
36 Causton Street
London SW1P 4ST
www.spck.org.uk

*British Library Cataloguing-in-Publication Data*
A catalogue record for this book is available from the British Library

ISBN 978–0–281–07776–2
eBook ISBN 978–0–281–07777–9

Typeset by Manila Typesetting Company
First printed in Great Britain by Jellyfish Print Solutions
Subsequently digitally reprinted in Great Britain

eBook by Manila Typesetting Company

Produced on paper from sustainable forests

*To Denise, Dawn and Sharon*
*May their love for the world always show*

Love all God's creation, the whole and every grain of sand in it. Love every leaf, every ray of God's light. Love the animals, love the plants, love everything. If you love everything, you will perceive the divine mystery in things . . . By loving, man gains new respect for everything in God's world. Thus we must love not occasionally, for a moment, but for ever.

(Fyodor Dostoevsky, *Brothers Karamazov*, Book 6, Chapter 3)

All things, there, are charged with love, are charged with God and if we know how to touch them give off sparks and take fire, yield drops and flow, ring and tell of him.

(Gerard Manley Hopkins in Christopher Devlin sj (ed.), *The Sermons and Devotional Writings of Gerard Manley Hopkins*, Oxford University Press, 1959, p. 195, see 'Introduction', note 2, p. 129)

 # Contents

# Contents

## WATER

## EARTH

## HUMANKIND

## CONCLUSION

#  *Acknowledgements*

I would like to thank the staff at SPCK for their help and support over many years, and I am especially grateful to Alison Barr for her guidance and friendship.

I am indebted to the many groups that have allowed me to experiment with prayer and ideas about God and creation, especially the churches of Castleton and Danby in North Yorkshire, and the church on Lindisfarne, with its multitude of visitors.

Finally, my utmost thanks and love to Denise, who has journeyed with me in expressing our love for the world.

*Introduction*

Have you ever suddenly been enraptured by creation? The world is full of wonders and invites us into realms of awe and adoration. Yet for us not only to behold but also *to be held* by creation in all its glory, we have to make ourselves available. We have to allow the world to speak to us. We have to tune in.

For so much of our lives, we are distracted. We may be living in the present but our minds have tended to race ahead, worrying about what is coming, or, when things are too difficult, retreating to comforting memories of the past. The great challenge is to learn to be still and make space in our lives for living in the now.

By the time we are grown, most of us have ceased to thrill at the dawn or the blackbird's song. We no longer stoop to enjoy the glory that is revealed in a flower or a butterfly, the intricate splendour of petal or wing. It is amazing how concerned we become with trivial matters, worries over mere nothings, when the glory of the world waits to speak to us. There is nothing in creation free from mystery if we look deep enough or long enough. Life takes place within the setting of a great miracle and we can derive endless delight from contemplation of it. Everything that is, is holy. We need to discover again that there is an adventure to be lived in our world, a personal discovery to be made of the presence and the life that dances in all things and to delight in joining in the dance.

One of my earliest remembrances of awe comes from when I was in junior school. I was standing beneath an ash tree in the spring, awestruck by its sheer presence. For a long time, I stared into its beautiful greening branches, just enjoying this strange connection with another piece of creation. Somehow, I was aware that it existed in its own right, that it had its own being. I could not find the words to explain this to two friends when they came by and wanted to know what I was looking at. They could not understand what I saw. They said it was 'only a tree'. They could not see the extra-ordinariness in it being what it was.

I was learning to love the world and the beauty and glory within it. Everything seemed full of life, full of radiance, forever offering something new.

At 16, spending my nights underground, it crossed my mind I was not much different from a mole as I sifted earth – or to be more precise coal dust – in the dark. I was working on my own under the head of a conveyor belt, and at three in the morning came the time to have a short break and eat my bait. I sat on the stone floor with my back to the wall of the tunnel in the usual, ordinary way. Then I looked above me and, behold, my world changed. For there over my head was a bed of hundreds of thousands of molluscs that had been fossilized in one of the great changes in our earth's climate. These once living creatures had rested here over millions of years and had never before been seen by the human eye. A thrill went through my whole being at the wonder of it all – the mystery of the beyond, the whisper of a presence greater than any molluscs. Though unable to express the experience or my feelings clearly, I knew then beyond doubt that the world is full of a vibrant mystery.

It was not long after this that I was grabbed again in completely different surroundings. We came out of the coal mine at eight in the morning and a few of us got on our bikes and started speeding home for breakfast. Near the bottom of a hill, I saw a sea of blue in the nearby wood. My workmates continued their journey but I had to stop. Leaving my bike by the verge of the road, I entered into the stillness of the place and beheld a world transfigured. It was more than a pulsing blue, changing with the breeze and the moving dappled light. This sea of flowers not only provoked a sense of awe and wonder, it conveyed something of the glorious power that fills our world. I wanted to capture its essence, to share it with my mother ill at home. So I took off my pit hat and filled it with bluebells, placed my hat safely in my bag and cycled the rest of my way. I found I could not explain the beauty or what it had made me feel. Indeed, I was a little sad to see my offering looked rather limp and droopy. Yet my mother was overjoyed at the gift.

Once the eyes of the heart are opened we look upon the world in a different way. Beauty can be revealed by the smallest things. Gerard Manley Hopkins made this entry in his notebook on 18 May 1870:

> One day when the bluebells were in bloom I wrote the following. I do not think I have seen anything more beautiful than the bluebell I have been looking at. I knew the beauty of our Lord by it.[1]

Much later, at college, I would read some more words from a sermon preached in 1881 by Gerard Manley Hopkins that perfectly expressed how I felt on each of these three occasions:

All things, there, are charged with love, are charged with God and if we know how to touch them give off sparks and take fire, yield drops and flow, ring and tell of him.[2]

I was slow to learn that it is in this world that we are to look for the Other, the numinous, the Presence of whom all creation speaks. The universe is a book about God. This concept goes back to at least the third century AD. When St Antony was asked how he managed without books, he responded: 'My book is the nature of created things, and as often as I have mind to read the words of God, they are at my hand.'

A little over a century later St Augustine would echo this idea. In one of his sermons he said:

Some people, in order to discover God, read books. But there is a great book: the very appearance of created things. Look above you! Look below you! Note it. Read it. God, whom you want to discover, never wrote that book with ink. Instead He set before your eyes the things He had made. Can you ask for a louder voice than that? What, heaven and earth shout to you, 'God made me!'[3]

Gregory of Nyssa, living in the fourth century, would echo this in a Catechetical Oration:

Who, studying the universe, would be so narrow in his thinking as not to believe that God is in everything, that he clothes himself with the universe, and that at one and the same time he both contains it and dwells in it? Everything that exists depends on the One who is, and nothing can exist except in the bosom of the One who is.

My final quote on this way of reading God's presence is commonly attributed to Meister Eckhart and is one of my favourites:

Apprehend God in all things,
for God is in all things,
every single creature is full of God
and is a book about God.
Every creature is a word of God.
If I spent enough time with even the tiniest of creatures –
even a caterpillar –
I would never have to prepare a sermon. So full of God
   is every creature.

I hope this book will help you enjoy and appreciate what is around you. Each section explores a part of the universe, offering a short meditation of the sort I often do, an exercise and a prayer.

At theological college in the 1950s, we were allotted a time for meditation each day. This normally lasted 20 minutes and focused on a word or passage from the Scriptures. I must admit my attention often wandered and needed to brought back. But for those who attended, the Scriptures could speak, help us be still and wait on God. When my mind was giddy with thoughts I would turn to St Francis's Canticle of the Creatures, which was on a card I kept in my Bible, and seek to give thanks and praise for creation. In case you are not familiar with it, here it is.

Most high, most powerful, good Lord God, to you
   belong praise, glory, honour and blessing!

Praise be my Lord God with all his creatures, and especially for our brother the sun,
who brings us the day and brings us the light: fair is he
and shines with great splendour.
O Lord he signifies you.
Praise be my Lord for our sister the moon and for the
stars,
which he has set clear and lovely in the heavens.
Praise be my Lord, for our brother the wind, and for
air and cloud, calms and all weather, by which you
uphold life in all creatures.
Praise be my Lord for our sister water, who is very ser-
viceable to us,
and humble, precious and pure.
Praise be my Lord for our brother fire through whom
you give light in darkness,
he is bright, pleasant, very mighty and strong.
Praise be my Lord for our mother the earth, who sustains us and keeps us,
and brings forth various fruits and flowers of many
colours and grass.
Praise and bless the Lord, and give thanks to him and
serve him with great humility.
Alleluia! Alleluia![4]

After a year of following this pattern, I decided I would meditate on something that was not from Scripture, a quote or
a poem that spoke strongly to me. Then, I added a third
dimension, meditating on something in creation. I would
take a leaf or a fossil, a piece of rock or a flower, and place it
before me and see what it could reveal to me. Then I extended

my scope again and decided to meditate each day upon the wider world and rejoice in the wonders of creation. More or less following the order from Genesis 1, I mapped out a rough guide.

| | |
|---|---|
| **Monday** | Explore the beginnings of No-thing, light out of darkness. |
| **Tuesday** | Rejoice in space, the sky, the clouds and the air. As you breathe, give thanks for your life. |
| **Wednesday** | Discover the properties of water, ice and snow. Rejoice in streams, rivers and seas, and the renewing power of the water cycle that refreshes the waters upon the earth. |
| **Thursday** | Wonder at the sun, moon and stars. Explore the mysteries of galaxies, day and night, tides and seasons. |
| **Friday** | Rejoice in all living things, plants, fish, birds, animals. Discover them in their diversity and individuality and preciousness; seek to see them as subjects in their own right. |
| **Saturday** | Enjoy your own humanity, your mystery of being. Explore the wonders of human life. Give your undivided attention to someone. Seek to treat everyone with awe and respect. |
| **Sunday** | Rejoice in the numinous mystery that is in all things as all are in the Presence that some of us call God. Rest within this mystery. |

St Francis's Canticle of the Creatures and my guide for meditating on something of creation led me to much that I have written in this book. Perhaps as an exercise you could devise your own guide for meditating on the world. Add to your prayers daily thanksgiving and praise for creation and your life within it.

But now let's go back to the beginning of time and space, as we explore the wonders and mysteries of our universe throughout the ages.

#  A new era

The world I was born into in the 1930s appeared to have altered little since the Middle Ages. Although great progress was being made in the fields of science and physics, life, seed time and harvest were much as they had always been. As the country recovered from the Second World War, however, new methods of communication, new discoveries and new machinery brought about change at an ever-increasing pace.

There have been many innovations in farming and land use. In 1947, Clement Attlee brought in the Price Support System for farmers, guaranteeing a fixed price for whatever they were growing. This made it profitable to plough up marginal land, scrubland and damp pastures. As a result, ditches and ponds were filled in and the water piped away; hedges were ripped out, and small woods and single trees disappeared; acidic land was heavily treated with lime. In eastern England, thousands of miles of hedgerows were lost, some of which were centuries old. Ancient orchards were torn out by the hundreds, destroying the nesting sites and food source of many birds. The traditional patchwork of fields disappeared in the creation of larger areas to grow wheat and other grain crops. All this was done with the financial encouragement of the Ministry of Agriculture. Farming was to be seen as a business and an industry and judged by how much it could get out of the land. The cost was a heavy toll on our flora and fauna.

The changes meant there was room for enormous new farm machinery. Farming communities were thinned out as one person and a machine could now do what used to take a team. The new farmer often worked alone all day inside the cab of a large tractor, listening to music on a headset.

Then came changes in the method of spring and autumn sowing. Autumn sowing meant the stubble was soon ploughed in, destroying a great food supply for the buntings and finches whose numbers quickly dwindled. Spring crops made it almost impossible for lapwings and skylarks to nest, and, if they did, it was likely their nests would be sprayed with chemicals and their young birds lost to machinery. The reduction of horses on farms meant there was no need for so many hay meadows, as cows are quite happy to eat the gunk called silage. So fields were ploughed and sown with a new variety of rye grass, which squeezed out many of our well-loved field flowers: hay meadows full of cornflowers, poppies, daisies, buttercups and many other species of flower disappeared. For this reason, rye grass has been designated by many as 'green concrete'. Hedgerows were slashed by machinery in the autumn, and as there were fewer berries for the birds, they were almost silent in winter. Next year the hawthorn hedgerows would not flower so well.

Nor did it end there. Massive ploughs break up fragile soil in a different way from the old horse-drawn ones. Fertilizers, pesticides and herbicides are used in gigantic quantities. And mistakes have been made. DDT followed by organo-chlorines not only kills insects but also kills birds that eat the poisoned insects. We rely on the bees to pollinate our flowers, fruit and crops. Yet our government continued the use of neonicotinoids for spraying the seeds of oil-seed rape for over a year before also banning its use on this crop, though it was already banned in the EU and the USA. Although these chemicals are still not yet banned completely, further restrictions have been agreed, so progress is being made. Initially, the chemical is applied to stave off pests such as aphids and root-eating grubs, but it remains in the plant as it grows and the bees harvesting the pollen will absorb the chemical that is harmful to them. We fail to realize our connectedness to all of creation. In the world at large, in the same time as our population has doubled, we have lost half of our biodiversity. Time and time again we ignore the fact we are part of the intricate web of life and if we harm something within that web we are harming or diminishing ourselves.

## New visions

### Our precious little planet

On Christmas Eve 1968, I had prepared a sermon on 'the Word was made flesh and dwelt among us'. Visiting a friend whose wife had gone into labour, I discovered they had already decided to call their child Hugo Apollo. For this was the night Apollo 8 went around the dark side of the moon and out of sight of planet earth. William Anders, Frank Bormann and Jim Lovell emerged from the Lunar Shadow and saw a crescent earth arising against the blackness of space. They chose as part of their message home the creation story from Genesis. A quarter of a million miles from earth, William Anders, the pilot, began:

We are now approaching lunar sunrise and, for all the people back on earth, the crew of Apollo 8 has this message that we would like to send to you.

In the beginning God created the heaven and the earth. And the earth was without form and void, and darkness was upon the deep. And the Spirit of the Lord moved upon the face of the waters. And God said let there be light: there was light. And God saw the light, that it was good, and God divided the light from the darkness.

On 24 December 1968, during the lunar orbit, the following conversation took place, which allows us to hear the astronauts' reaction on seeing the earth:

ANDERS  Oh my God! Look at that picture over there! There's the Earth coming up. Wow, is that pretty.

BORMAN  (joking) Hey, don't take that, it's not scheduled.

ANDERS  (laughs) You got a colour film, Jim? Hand me that roll of colour quick, would you . . .

LOVELL  Oh man, that's great!

Anders found a suitable camera and took a photograph, later released by NASA, which became known as *Earthrise*. It shows how alone the earth is in the darkness of space, how beautiful and fragile it looks. Then almost 40 years later, on 16 July 2015, NASA released a view of the earth from the dark side of the moon. How brilliant and alive the earth looks in comparison with the barrenness of the moon. These photos help us see our world from a new perspective.

There has been great progress in our scientific understanding of the origin and make-up of our world. We need to open our eyes to the implications of the Big Bang and of quantum physics – which offer us a new vision of the universe – and to help people see that the ultimate mysteries of life are to be discovered all around us and *within each of us too*. We can rejoice in such new discoveries and allow them to enrich our faith.

## The Big Bang

The Big Bang takes us back before the creation of the universe to the beginning of time and space. We move beyond language and understanding to the mysterious source of all that exists – a numinous power impossible to comprehend though not impossible to apprehend. We cannot explain this source of being, which we may or may not choose to call God, but we are all involved in the mystery, for each of us carries it within us: it shapes our being. And as all that exists comes from this Originating Power, so we discover all things are related, from galaxies to geese, from stars to shrimps, from planets to people: nothing stands alone. We are even related to the wheat of the field from which we get our daily bread; we share ancestral enzymes, which proves the point.

The more we look at our universe, the more we see how wonderful that creative power is in the shaping of all things. This is a place where choice is possible, and we can rejoice in the freedom we are given.

## Quantum

The most important aspect of the quantum principle is this: we do not stand outside the universe as observers. We are not separate from it at all but a part of it and all our actions have an impact. Let's say we sought to look at and measure something as small as an electron. Taking that measurement would affect the electron, which would have a knock-on effect on the universe. All things are hitched to other things. We are part of a great web of action and reaction. Nothing stands alone: all that is influences other things. The strands of the web are innumerable and often almost invisible, thinner than gossamer. But touch one bit of the web and it reverberates; act and the whole universe responds.

Quantum physics reveals that nothing we look upon is solid, that solidity is an illusion. Everything, including ourselves, is made up of a collection of atoms that whirl around in a dance of pure energy.

The Big Bang and the quantum principle have great implications for how we should look at the world.

## Sacred

There is nothing so ordinary that God cannot be revealed through it. However, God leaves you room to recognize him or not, to seek him or not. Though God is a hidden God, he has not gone into hiding but speaks to us through his world. This is where we meet him, and in our encounters the ordinary has the capacity to become extraordinary. Indeed, nothing is truly secular, for holiness permeates all if we would only acknowledge this.

We cannot divide the world up into what is sacred and what is not, for all comes from the Originating Source and contains the mystery of that source within. All things are worthy of adoration, awe and reverence. If this doesn't seem to be the case, then we have not looked deep enough. Too often we relegate God and the kingdom of heaven to the far distance, when God and the kingdom are close at hand. There really is no need to go in search of God for, in the words of St Paul, 'In him we live and move and have our being' (Acts 17.28.) It is important to speak to him, listen to him and speak about him.

When we discover the presence of God, we see all things in their depth and beauty. But if we ignore the presence that vibrates in every atom, we will live a lie and become lonely and alone. If our deep sense of loss is shared by everyone around us, then there is a danger we will accept our blindness for normality. We need to hear the call to thrust out a little, to become more sensitive, more alive to what is around us. We may have to turn our backs on our normal routine for a while, but the reward for doing so will be to discover a depth to life that has been passing us by. Everything that is, is full of mystery, everything is holy. Nothing is profane; all is sacred, for all belongs to God. We must learn again to stop and to give our wholehearted attention to this wonderful world in which we live, and let it reveal the mysterious presence within it.

Too often we have separated things as if they stood on their own, whereas in reality all things are linked. Body, mind and spirit *together* make up our whole being. When the Hebrew people talked of the soul, that's what they meant. Dualism is a dangerous concept, which splits body from spirit and heaven from earth. Religion should not be set against science, matter against spirit; we need both/and (not either/or) – and, of course, the 'something else' at work that is beyond description.

This world is very much a place where I feel at home and I want no other! But over the years I have thrilled to find this visible world is interwoven with another strand I am still only slowly becoming aware of. I do not want to call it another world or even another kingdom, for that implies separation and the dangers of dualism. But in fact heaven and earth are one: God's rule of love is here and now. The kingdom of God is part and parcel of this world. In reality it is better to say this world in which we live is part of God's kingdom. And as people of this world, we are children of God, living in his presence, experiencing his love. The material and the spiritual are woven finely together and quite inseparable. The visible world of matter and the invisible world of spirit are not two worlds but one. We belong to both, here and now. For simplicity, I could say we are people of two realms, of two kingdoms, the interplay of which is vital to our well-being. This is not to deny a life beyond this world, beyond what we call death. But if life is eternal we are already in it! Eternity does not come after death, though clearer vision and a fuller life may. If there is eternal life, it has begun. We can live in the eternal now! Rather than juggle with the idea of two kingdoms, why not seek to make yourself at home in the world that God has given you? Here you will find the Other, who is in this world, and in you.

## Communion

I would like us to think more deeply about our common union. In a sense, we cannot go to communion, make our communion or receive our communion, for we are already in common union with God, and through God in common union with all creation. We dwell in him, as does the tiniest atom, cell or element. All matter is incarnate and holy. The universe is the Word made flesh. Yet the God who is present in all transcends all, is beyond all and cannot be confined by any single thing.

We need to celebrate that we dwell in him and he in us. The mind cannot grasp this fully, nor will we ever comprehend it (for no one can see God). But it is possible to apprehend God, to catch glimpses of his glory and grandeur. The Church's hugely exciting task is to help people to open their eyes and their hearts to their common union with God and his universe.

Despite what I said about communion above, I am not suggesting that there is no need for sacraments. Sacraments cannot be explained. They are about hidden grace and the unseen love and presence of God. They are designed to bring us before the Great Other and help us grasp that we are immersed in him. Words cannot explain what happens in this encounter, for it is living and ever changing. But it can be experienced, enjoyed and celebrated. Presence, hope, healing, wholeness and holiness are all gifts offered to us.

A ballerina was once asked what a particular dance meant and replied, 'If I could have said it, I would not have the need to dance it.' Like a hug or a kiss, sacraments can say more than a thousand words.

## Exercise

Find a quiet place and give thanks for the beginning of creation and the creating source that indwells all, including you.

## Prayer

We rejoice in our common union with our Creating God,
and our common union with creation.
We accept the world from you, O God,
and from the world the revealing of your presence.
Lord, may we present you to the world
and offer your world in praise to you.
We give thanks that consecration and
communion are your gifts to all.

# IN THE BEGINNING

# 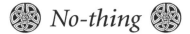 *No-thing*

The universe has its origin in the uncreated. The uncreated brought forth all that there is, all that there ever will be. All being comes from a singular gift out of No-thing. There is nothing in the entire universe – from neutron to nebula, from element to elephant, from galaxy to gazelle, from planet to person – that does not contain within itself the mystery of this uncreated source.

The power that caused the universe to come into being is beyond space and time, for space and time began with creation, as the particles moved outwards. Describing this source as No-thing shows the limits of our language and our comprehension. There have been many attempts through the ages to name and explain what happened, and it is right for us to try to do so, as long as we remember that all images are only pointers to a greater reality: the mystery of the Presence that dwells in all, as all dwell within the Presence.

It is interesting that the language of the scientist and physicist in this regard is as mystical as that of the theologian.

**No-thing**

Creation from nothing
No-thing
No name
Uncreated
Beyond reason
Transcendent

The ground of our being
The beyond
And yet – within
The Jews said there could be no image
YHWH is only a symbol.
Beyond words
He who knows does not name
He who names does not know
Beyond our control
Not to be held
Nor to be confined
Not male or female
Nor creature
Nor object
Untouchable
Yet touching all things
Beyond comprehension
But not beyond apprehension.

**Exercise**

The Originating Source is a mystery to be enjoyed. Rejoice that you are born of a mysterious source, as is all creation, and that your life contains that mystery within. You may like to choose a subject to look at and to appreciate its mystery of being.

**Prayer**

O God incomprehensible, we apprehend you.
O God invisible, we behold you.
O God mysterious, we know you.

*No-thing*

O God untouchable, we hold you.
You speak to us through your creation
For you are the source of all there is
And in you all have their being.
Glory be to you, O God.

# *Fiery furnace*

What we now know of the beginning of the universe is awesome and full of mystery. We have discovered that it is about 13.7 billion years old and 93 billion light years across. The first stars appeared about 100 million years after the Big Bang. The universe contains at least 100 billion galaxies and each galaxy contains hundreds of billions of stars. Yet all of this came from something far smaller than a single atom, its density and heat beyond comprehension.

In a moment of glory, in a blinding radiance too swift to capture, the Big Bang took place and a universe of endless possibilities was born. In less than a minute it was 1 million billion miles across and still growing. The temperature is thought to have been 1,000 trillion trillion degrees centigrade. Yet within a second it had dropped to a heat of about 10 billion degrees. The lighter elements were created – mainly hydrogen and helium with a dash of lithium (about one atom in 100 million) and beryllium. In the time it takes to boil an egg, the universe had four distinct forces, gravity, strong and weak nuclear forces and electromagnetism, and was composed of around 75 per cent hydrogen and 25 per cent helium. The potential for your creation – and 98 per cent of all the matter of the universe there is or ever will be – was there in that quantum leap of glory out of No-thing.

## The package

If we had been there, the package was
so small we could not have seen it
so hot we would not dare approach it
so heavy nothing could lift it.
No one could guess what it contained.
But, the Creator of all knew.
It was his gift.
With almighty power he opened it
and the universe was sown.
The first seeds were tiny but full of power.
They produced the atom and in time the ants,
they produced the elements and later the elephants,
they produced the stars and long after the seas,
they produced the galaxies and, eventually, the gazelles,
they produced the planets and, ages after, the plankton.
All in their own good time, in their uniqueness:
all in God's plan for the world, for you and me.

## Exercise

Though we know a lot about the beginning of the universe,
the speeds, the temperatures and the distances are all too
much to take in. We might ponder instead how creative those
first few seconds were – without that creativity, you would
not be here or reading this page! Rejoice in your being, for
that is a wonder in itself.

**Prayer**

Lord, I arise today through your gift of life.
Through the mystery of creation,
The Big Bang,
Splendour of fire,
The expanding universe,
The shaping of galaxies,
The birth of the solar system,
Light of sun,
Radiance of moon,
The fecundity of earth,
Through your love and life-giving power,
I arise today.

# ✺ *Quantum mechanics* ✺

Quantum mechanics is about how the elements work at subatomic level. Here we enter into mystery, for not only is this a world we cannot see or touch, it is one that does not follow the laws of motion as we have understood them since Newton. It appears that there is an indeterminacy, a fluidity, at the heart of all things. The universe is not a mechanism, like a clock that is wound up and allowed to run but, rather, has a part to play in its own creation. The future is not as predictable as some imagine. There are opportunities for adjustments in direction. Nothing is planned out in a fixed rigid pattern; rather, within the balance of things, there is freedom for development and change. There is no bullet with your name on it, no fixed time for you to die.

Particles appear to exist only in relationship. Electrons only exist when they interact with something. Is it not surprising that as yet no one fully understands quantum mechanics? What we can be sure of is that all events in creation are relational and linked to others; nothing stands alone. Everything shares a common union and a common source that is beyond description.

## Creative freedom

I rejoice in the glorious freedom of creation.
Nothing is determined by fate.
There is opportunity to change,

freedom to choose
and the surprise of chance
which contributes to life in wide array.
The universe is full of diversity:
stars differ from stars in glory,
and relationships affect our choices,
so that no two creatures are the same.
Each rose has its own shape and scent;
each tree its own beauty;
each cheerful sparrow its own charm.
Over the ages creation has ensured
that no thing is a copy of another:
every snowflake a masterpiece,
every person unique.

## Exercise

The subatomic world is a place we cannot see or touch, but we can learn a lot from it. Nothing stands alone; all exists in connection with the rest of the universe. Your life is made up of endless relationships and your actions affect others more than you may realize. Consider this and think about how you might behave more lovingly in your home and in the world at large.

There are times when we do not appreciate the fragile beauty around us. Taking the miracle of our life for granted seems to be the natural human state. But if we become too blasé we lose perspective on who we are and our place within the world.

## Prayer

Lord God, you have given us the glorious freedom, built into your creation, to choose and to be creative. Teach us to use our freedom rightly and with wisdom for the benefit of all, to your glory.

#  *The elements*

A millionth of a second after the Big Bang, when the quarks had cooled enough to be bonded together by the strong nuclear force to form protons and neutrons, hydrogen, the first of the chemical elements, was created from one proton and one neutron. Within three minutes, the universe was cool enough for protons and neutrons to unite to form helium with two protons and one or two neutrons. There was also a small amount of lithium with three protons, and beryllium with four protons, the third and fourth simplest elements. I spoke earlier of the four distinct forces that we know of today: gravity, strong and weak nuclear forces and electromagnetism. Gravity was at work to gather the hydrogen and helium into great clouds. Then for 100 million years it became dark; it was as if everything just stopped for a long time. However gravity was still busily drawing the billions of atoms in each cloud tighter together until they were compressed into stars – and there was light! The universe became radiant as the primary stars were born.

Behind the abounding diversity of our world there is an amazing simplicity and nowhere is that more obvious than in the making of the elements. To create the elements it would seem all you need is hydrogen, gravity and the right conditions, which include the creativity of the mysterious power within all.

## Gravity

Gravity is the weakest of the four forces.

Yet gravity caused the speed of expansion to slow down.

Gravity prevented things running off at such a pace that nothing would come together.

Yet gravity did not impose so strong a regime on the universe that it imploded back upon itself.

The weakest of the forces caused the gases to come together in great clouds:

in its own good time, it made billions of stars to shine and as many galaxies to take shape.

Gravity shaped the universe and caused stars to live and die.

After aeons of time it created the solar system with its star, the sun,

and the planets, including planet earth.

Gravity causes the tides of our oceans,

and water to flow in our rivers and streams.

It has shaped the landscape and built the mountains.

It has created the wing of the bird and the muscles of a man that they may live in creative tension.

Gravity is a great instrument in the shaping of all things;

a great gift issuing out of No-thing.

## Exercise

The wonderful creative power of the beginning is quite mind-boggling. Rejoice that this brought the universe into being, has been at work through all the ages to shape our universe, and makes it possible for you and me to live here on earth.

## Prayer

Lord of the elements, glory to you for the creation of all that exists from what seemed the simplest beginnings. The wonderful diversity of the universe comes from the working of gravity and your creative power, from the first tiny atoms to superstars and mighty galaxies and the boundless regions of space. All of creation comes from you and reveals your presence to those who open their eyes and their hearts. Glory to you, Lord.

#  *Space*

Look at the sky at night. What do you see? Ursa Major, Orion, the moon, the planets . . . But if you cease naming and simply behold, there are objects and a vast emptiness . . . an emptiness that should fill us with awe. Look long enough at space, and something within you resonates. Space is an important element of being; it is necessary for anything to survive. No two objects can fill the same space and each object's space is precious to its being. None can exist without space.

Physicists have discovered that the 'solidity' of matter is an illusion created by our senses. In fact 99.9 per cent is 'empty' space, such as the space between atoms compared with their size, with as much space again in each atom. The atoms of our body make us like a great galaxy of more space than stars. Yet our spacious body constitutes life in all its fullness. It is a microcosm of the macrocosm that is the universe.

When you learn about the distances in space for the first time it should be exciting. Light travels at a constant speed of 186,000 miles per second – one second from earth to moon; eight minutes from sun to earth. Our next nearest neighbouring star in space is Proxima Centuri and it takes 4.5 years before its light reaches earth. The light from the Andromeda Galaxy, the galaxy next to ours, takes 2.4 million years to reach us. When we look at it, we can look back in time!

## We all need space

Once everyone was able to look upon great spaces,
yet many have adapted to limited space:
small houses and small rooms,
narrow streets and tiny gardens –
vision is restricted.
We all need space
in which to move,
to breathe, to think,
to work, to play.
We all need to be able to stand in our own space.
Yet now people are afraid of space.
They fill it with sound,
with words
with possessions.
Our lives are overcrowded,
over stimulated, over filled.
Space is seen as emptiness,
as blank,
as nothing.
Yet it gives everything its shape.
We need to learn to live in our space,
to renew our being,
to find peace of mind,
to extend our vision,
to hear and be touched by beauty.
God loves space:
he made so much of it.

## Exercise

Go out on a starry night and see if you can find a dark area, or go to one of the many observatory centres that give you a chance to view the stars through a telescope. Enjoy the grandeur and the majesty of it all. Then spend some time meditating on how each star needs space to exist; on how space is precious to every creature, including you.

## Prayer

To you, O God, belong praise and glory for the majesty of the
    starlit heavens and the mightiness of space.
You give space to each creature that exists.
You have given us the space in which to move and to think.
May we not overcrowd this space or infringe the space of
    other beings.
And may we make sure we keep a space in our lives for you
    and your love.
Blessed are you, Lord God of all creation.

 *Stars*

We have learned how the stars were made. Almost simultaneously, billions lit up and their glory filled the heavens as they sparkled like diamonds in a sea of darkness.

Stars are grouped in galaxies. We live in the Milky Way Galaxy of around 400 billion stars. The Andromeda is a giant galaxy of a trillion stars and is about 220,000 light years across. The Orion Nebula is 24 light years across: a light year is six trillion miles, so that is 144 trillion miles. The Pleiades, one of the nearest star clusters to earth, is 400 light years away. Our nearest star is the sun at a mere 93 million miles away.

These figures are overwhelming and hard to comprehend, but they give us a feel of the vastness of space and the multitude of stars.

Stars live and die. A new star is born most years within the Milky Way, and smaller stars live for billions of years. They shine by burning up their hydrogen. When this is done, the star turns from hydrogen to the helium it has produced for its fuel by nuclear fusion. When this is used up, it turns to the carbon it has produced, and then to the oxygen. This action of using and producing elements will continue until it has produced the first 25 of the elements known in the universe. After billions of years, the star's available resources are used up, and when the core has been transformed to iron, it is unstable. The outer layer explodes, hurling the precious elements in outward layers into space to create a planetary nebula. Such stars will end their days as a white dwarf – but do not be deceived by the name, for they will probably still be as big as earth. The creation of carbon and oxygen are good news for us, for they are needed in our make-up and the make-up of many plants and creatures upon earth. But if it stopped there we would never have had our being: for that we need something else – a superstar.

## Under a starlit sky

Dazzling diamond light
in the dark before the morn,
numinous nebula where stars are born,
and swirling galaxies where they die.
Tonight, it is a peaceful sky
of space beyond comprehension,
of stars beyond calculation.
But have you learned to look in awe?
Stars are wonders;
every single one a powerhouse.
Changing hydrogen to helium,
then through each element,
all the way to uranium.
Creating what we need for life
out of their devastation.
Gaseous globes giving birth
as the sun blesses earth.

## Exercise

Look up on a starlit night and allow yourself to be part of the magnificent universe, with space beyond quantifying and stars too many to number. Just enjoy the night air. Look at the great sweep of the Milky Way, and the patterns of constellations, and absorb the beauty and awesomeness of this great expanse. Think how it reveals the mighty power and wonderful creativity of the Originating Source. Perhaps see if you can share this night of wonder with a friend, loved one or child.

## Prayer

Blessed are you, Lord God of all creation,
you created the stars and gave each one its glory.
We give you thanks for starlight,
for illumination that guides us in times of darkness.
We give you thanks for sunlight
that brings warmth and life to our world.
We give you thanks for moonlight
and for all who reflect the light of your presence.
Blessed are you, Lord God, giver of light and love.

#  Superstars

A superstar (or supernova) is much larger than a normal star, and the bigger it is, and the brighter it shines, the sooner it burns out: the most massive stars may burn up their hydrogen in only a few million years. One such superstar is Betelgeuse, a red giant thought to be 500 million miles in diameter, which is about 20 times the diameter of our sun. It is the brightest star in Orion's belt and the ninth brightest we can see – a mere 500 light years away.

After millions or several billion years, when the superstar has used up its resources as far as iron, then due to what we call quantum mechanics it will produce the highest temperatures ever known to form all the natural elements in the universe. Carbon fuses with helium to create neon, neon fuses with helium to make magnesium, and so the alchemy continues until the other 72 elements have been created. The superstar then collapses inwards and a shockwave shoots outwards with a resulting explosion.

The superstar is the great alchemist, for at this point wave after wave of elements – carbon, nitrogen, oxygen, tungsten, copper, vanadium and so on – are thrown out to seed new worlds. For example, it creates calcium, needed for bones, and phosphorus, needed for photosynthesis. In the galaxies where atoms of the new elements swirl across space, second- and third-stage stars will eventually come into being. The explosion of a superstar makes way for new creations and new possibilities.

About four and a half billion years ago, such a superstar explosion brought about the creation of our solar system, then life on earth. If you want to trace your family tree as far back as possible, you can say, 'I was born of an exploding star!'

## Superstars

Giants of the galaxies,
short-lived among the stars:
only a few billion years!
You share with the Creator
in making new beings possible.
In your death you beget a family:
stars arise out of your dust,
your atoms seed the universe,
floating in space they create anew.
From you planet earth gave birth to creatures,
and in time to all human beings.
I am related to you as are all on earth.
We belong to one great family.
In the universe nothing is lost,
only changed, transfigured.
Nothing is discarded,
only transformed and born anew.
The creative power cares for us all.

## Exercise

Have another night under the stars. Have you ever noticed how they move? How some are not visible to us at certain times of the year? See what phase the moon is in, though a moonless night is best for viewing the stars. If you live in the northern hemisphere you should be able to pick out Orion and the superstar Betelgeuse. Enjoy the glory of it all.

## Prayer

Lord God, Creator of all, teach us to wonder.
Open our eyes to the glory of your creation.
Open our minds to the awesomeness of the night sky.
Open our hearts to the love that sustains all creation
and enfolds each one of us, day by day.

#  Sun

I watch the sun rise out of the sea most days, sometimes golden, at other times a radiant red. Something happens to our inner being as the darkness is scattered by its glorious light.

One ordinary star among the 200 billion in our galaxy means everything to us. The sun is not only a light-giver but a life-giver. The sun's power controls everything from planets to plants to people. In many ways it is a mystery and the strangest place in our solar system.

The universe is 13.75 billion years old and the sun has been around about a third of that time. Around 5 billion years ago, a supernova exploded and scattered its debris far and wide, but the power of gravity not only held the debris in check, it helped over 99 per cent of it to come together to form the sun. From the other 1 per cent the planets were created. The sun's diameter is a hundred times that of the earth and this immensity gives it power over the rest of the solar system within the reach of its gravity.

Every second, through nuclear fusion on an unimaginable scale, the sun burns several hundred million tons of hydrogen, converting it to helium. If the sun were consuming hydrogen at a lesser rate, we would not get the required warmth to support life. As it is, it produces 400 million million million million watts of energy every *second*, equivalent to a million times the power consumption of the United States every *year*. This energy is the source of nearly all life on earth. For example, it is due to the sun that rivers flow. Photons travel 93 million miles from the sun to earth in about eight minutes. Through them the sun's power lifts every molecule of water in every river, in every cloud, in every raindrop, and this movement gives shape and colour to our earth, to go alongside the warmth and light we also receive.

**The sun**

St Francis saw the sun as an icon of God,
for the sun gives us life and light.
Every second the sun transforms millions of tons of its being
into light,
which travels to earth, dispelling darkness and bringing
forth life.
The plants, the herbs, the grass, the grain,
the fruit and the vegetables all absorb this energy into their
being.
They all exist due to the light of the sun.
The cattle that graze, the birds that feed on seeds and grains,
they all exist due to the light of the sun.
The wild creatures of the forests that walk or crawl,
they all exist due to the light of the sun.
For four million years, humans have been feasting on the
sun's energy:
through vegetables, fruit, grain and meat we get fuel to survive.
We exist due to the light of the sun.
With St Francis we say,
'Praise God for our brother the sun,
Who brings us the day and bring us the light,
Fair is he and shines with great splendour.'

## Exercise

If possible, go and watch a sunrise or sunset. Consider that all life on earth depends on the sun. You depend on it for your well-being. Take some time to explore in the sunlight the sun's gifts to us: light and colour and our daily bread are all dependent on the sun. When we eat fruit, vegetables and meat, we are eating the energy of the sun that they have absorbed. Rejoice in the wonderful relationships we can explore through the sun's light.

## Prayer

Creator God, as the sun rises we give you thanks for the gift
    of this new day,
for light, for colour, for our eyesight.
We give thanks that plants absorb the sun's energy
and in turn feed us with their gift from the sun.
Help us to appreciate the wonderful relationship between all
    created things,
Lord of all, and to tread gentle on the earth.

#  *Moon*

There are many moons in the solar system: Jupiter has 63, Neptune, 13, Mars, two tiny moons, and the earth only one. No other planet in the solar system has a moon as big in relation to its parent planet as we have: its diameter is a quarter of the earth's. Our moon is the fifth largest of those in our solar system, after Titan, Ganymede, Calisto and Io. It is almost close enough to us for us to be dubbed a double-planet system.

When the earth was quite young, about 4.5 billion years ago, it was still being bombarded by all sorts of debris from within the solar system. It was possibly then that the moon was created. It is thought a Mars-size planet came close enough to earth to give it a glancing blow, blasting rock and dust into an orbit around the earth, and that this gradually condensed to form the moon we see today. The theory is based on the fact that the moon is very similar in composition to the earth's outer crust, though less dense because its iron core is much smaller. Thus, its gravitation field is only about a sixth of the earth's – not really strong enough to hold on to an atmosphere.

Due to gravity, the moon causes two bulges in the earth's oceans, one on the side facing the moon and the other on the side opposite. This causes elevated sea levels called oceanic tides. As the earth spins on its axis, one of the ocean bulges (high tide) is held in place 'under' the moon, while another such tide is opposite. As a result, there are two high tides and two low tides in about 24 hours. Since the moon is orbiting the earth in the same direction as the earth's rotation, the high tides occur about every 12 hours and 25 minutes. The sun has a tidal effect on the earth, but its forces of attraction are only 40 per cent that of the moon's; the interplay of the sun and the moon is responsible for spring and neap tides.

The moon's gravity helps to stabilize the earth and to stop it wobbling like a top. This in turn helps to keep the seas calm and to regulate the seasons. It is thought the moon played an important role in the creation of life on earth, though its pull upon human beings is too small to have any marked effect.

## Moon

You who have no light of your own,
brighten up our night
with your soft radiance,
reflected from the bright sun,
illuminating the sky when day is done.
You bring stability to the earth,
stop the seas from slopping about,
give them their rise and fall.
You who have no life of your own
played a part in the creation of life on earth
and help the seasons come and go.
Your rhythm affects breeding animals,
the menstrual cycle keeps lunar time:
Great Barrier Reef coral sperm
at the first full moon of spring,
crabs and oysters react to the tide

even when taken out of the sea!
And yet there are some who malign you,
suggesting you drive people mad
when in fact you give stability.
Francis called you Sister Moon.
Did he perceive we are related?

## Exercise

Seek an opportunity to view the full moon. Be grateful for
its reflected light. You might like to learn which is a waxing
and which is a waning moon. A moonlight walk is always
something special. Go out with a loved one or help a child to
discover the loveliness of a moonlit night.

## Prayer

Blessed are you, Lord and Creator of light,
for bright sunshine that brings in the day,
awakening us to newness of life,
for starlight filling the darkness with wonder,
for the soft reflected glow of the moon
that is a beautiful gift to our earth.
May we praise and reflect
your light in our hearts and lives,
blessed Lord and Creator.

# ATMOSPHERE

#  *Air*

There are some things we take for granted until we are deprived of them. We could last without food for over three weeks, and without water for three days. But we could only last without air for three minutes. We live and move in air; it is all around us and within us.

The last 50 years of space exploration have uncovered worlds of intense heat and intense cold, worlds ablaze and worlds frozen. Within our own solar system there are inhospitable planets, places sculpted by intense pressure and others where violent storms have raged for hundreds of years. Amid all this harshness sits planet earth in comparative calm. Yet all that protects us from the extremes of heat and cold is a thin blue line we call our atmosphere. Thanks to this encircling mixture of gases, which is kept in place through gravity, we have air to breathe and water to drink and an earth fit for life. The atmosphere acts like a blanket to keep us warm and a shield to protect us from radiation.

Over the past century, greenhouse gases and other air pollutants have been causing problems for our planet. We've struggled with acid rain, ozone holes and climate change because we're disrupting the balance of our home. The atmosphere of earth is made up of a mixture of nitrogen (78 per cent), oxygen (21 per cent), and argon (almost 1 per cent) with only traces of other gases (0.039 per cent). In all, we are surrounded by 5 million billion tonnes of air.

The atmosphere is thickest near the surface of the earth and thins out with height until it eventually merges with space. The atmosphere is described as having five layers. Most of the weather and clouds are found in the first layer, the troposphere in which we dwell, which contains half of the earth's atmosphere. The next level is the stratosphere, where many jets choose to fly because it is very stable and the ozone layer absorbs harmful rays from the sun. Meteors or rock fragments burn up in the mesosphere. The thermosphere is a layer with auroras. It is also where the space shuttles orbit. The extremely thin exosphere is where the upper limit of our atmosphere merges into space.

Weather is the state of the atmosphere at a given time and place. As I said, most weather takes place in the troposphere, the lowest layer of the atmosphere. When meteorologists are compiling a weather report, they will include air and pressure, the amount and type of precipitation, the strength and direction of wind, and a description of the clouds.

Weather changes each day because the air in our atmosphere is always moving, redistributing energy from the sun. In most places in the world, the type of weather events expected vary through the year as seasons change. While weather can change rapidly, climate changes slowly, over decades or more, in response to alterations in the factors that determine our climate.

**Atmosphere**

Clouds, over a grey ocean,
displaying silver and gold,
drifting gently southwards.

As the earth spins,
why does it not leave them behind?
Why do they not go westward
as we turn to the east?
They belong to our world,
floating in their own sea:
part of the atmosphere.
Our natural home
is as much a part of the world as the oceans.
As fish need the waters,
so we need air
to fill our lungs
and refresh our being.
The atmosphere is not just any group of gases:
it is the life breath of the planet,
produced by numberless organisms
as they inhale and exhale.
An icon of another presence,
within us and about
in which we live and move and have our being.

## Exercise

We are becoming more aware of how as humans we are in danger of changing our atmosphere. Take a few deep breaths and be grateful for the air you breathe. Spend some time considering how you might reduce your carbon footprint. See if you can reduce how often you use your car, take holidays that involve flying or other ways you consume anything that pollutes the earth. We cannot say we love the world if we continue to despoil it.

## Prayer

God, our Creator, teach us to love
not only other people but all living creatures.
Teach us to love all green and growing things.
Teach us to love the air, the soil, the water.
God, our Creator, help us learn to work in harmony,
to avoid exploiting or misusing your creation.
God, our Creator, show us ways of not polluting
the land, the air, the waters.
God, our Creator, guide us in preserving species so other
  generations
may regard their beauty with wonder and awe.

#  Clouds

I have lived in the clouds and walked through them, so some attached to my clothes and some dampened my hair, and they all appeared grey. Then I left the clouds behind and ascended by car up on to a moorland ridge. Looking to where I had been, the clouds had changed colour for they were now white and fluffy. Yet, I knew if I went back they would be grey. I have also flown up through dark clouds into the sunlight and when I looked down upon them they were white. I have watched a new ploughed field after a rain shower and seen it steam like a boiling kettle, and on a frosty morning, a fence smoking in the sunlight as if on fire. On both these occasions, I was experiencing the potential beginning of a cloud.

Clouds form when an area of moist warm air rises and then begins to expand and cool. It will continue to do so until its temperature is the same as that which surrounds it. As it cools, the water vapour in the air condenses to form tiny droplets of water, which are the basic material of clouds. There are several factors that influence and affect cloud formation, with the sun and the wind playing a major part.

Cloud names often describe their appearance. There are four main types. 'Cumulus' means 'heap' and these are large white clouds with a flat base giving a heaped-up and fluffy appearance. Much higher cirrus clouds – 'cirrus' is Latin for a curl of hair – are fine and curly and composed of ice. The zone between cloud and air is not so clear, which makes them blurry at the edges. Stratus clouds are spread out in layers, the sort that often give complete cloud cover. 'Nimbus', though it just means cloud, is used to describe rain clouds. The four terms can be combined to describe nearly every shape and size of cloud, such as stratocumulus, cirrostratus or cumulo-nimbus, which is a heaped-up rain cloud.

It is good to appreciate the various clouds and their work in the watering of the earth.

## Clouds

Shape shifters
of many colours,
born of sun and water,
carrying parts of the sea.
Moving puddles
of yesterday
and returning them
again, in fresh showers
to clean and
water the earth.
Drifting in the air,
rising and falling again,
capable of mighty acts
like lightning strike.
Offering us storm,
wind and rain,
hail and snow.
Beauty of shape,
shelter from heat,
creator of wind,

part of a precious cycle
of our atmosphere,
living in a fine
and fragile balance.

## Exercise

Go out and take notice of the clouds, watching their movement and changing shape. You might like to learn the basic names for types of cloud.

Realize how precious they are in recycling the water that brings us our rain and snow.

If there is anything in the way you live that is harmful to climate, consider how you might change it.

## Prayer

Blessed are you, Lord God, for the atmosphere which surrounds us, for the air we breathe,

for the winds that blow, and the clouds that bring us rain to keep our land fresh and fertile.

As we watch the ever-changing climate, may we understand that we live within it and affect it.

Help us improve our relationship and walk gently upon the earth.

Blessed are you, Lord God Creator of all. Blessed are you for ever.

#  *Wind*

The wind is something we know only by its actions. We can feel a gentle breeze or protect ourselves against a stormy gale; we can see the action of the wind as it moves over a field of grain or shakes the branches of a tree. We can capture its power to drive a sailing boat along, to fly a kite or glider. But we cannot see it at all.

When the sun is clipping in and out of clouds, it can cause the wind to blow because it is creating pockets of hot and cold air. The main cause of wind is temperature, that is, the differences in temperature between different areas.

The gases that make up our atmosphere react to changes in temperatures. When gases warm up, atoms and molecules move quickly, spread out and rise. When air is cold, they move slowly and closer together and sink. Where air is rising we see lower pressure at the earth's surface, and where it is sinking we see higher pressure. In fact if it weren't for this rising and sinking motion in the atmosphere, then not only would we have no wind, but we would also have no weather. You might think that the warm air would lead to a higher-pressure area, but the opposite is true. Because warm air rises, it leaves behind an area of low pressure.

The sun warms up the air, but it does so unevenly. It hits different parts of the earth at different angles and, because the earth has oceans, mountains and other features, some places are warmer than others, giving us pockets of warm air and cold air.

This rising and sinking of air in the atmosphere takes place on both a global and a local scale. One of the simplest examples of a local wind is the sea breeze. On sunny days during the summer, the sun's rays heat the ground quickly. By contrast, the sea surface has a greater capacity to absorb the sun's rays and is more difficult to warm. This leads to a temperature contrast between the warm land and the cooler sea. A pressure difference is set up, and air moves inland from the sea to try and equalize this difference – making the sea breeze. It explains why beaches can be cooler than inland areas on a hot, sunny day.

**Wind**

Wind running on the waves,
wild:
whipping up the sea,
creating white horses,
blowing the foam at me,
you're having a spree.

Wind, sensual in the barley,
wanton:
teasing out the women's hair,
caressing their skin,
blowing their skirts about,
you're having an affair.

Wind whistling in the trees,
wilful:
making them sing,
stripping the leaves,

bringing in winter,
you're having a fling.

Wind moving in the city,
way-hay!
tearing down streets,
tossing rubbish about,
wobbling park seats,
you're having a treat!

## Exercise

Go out and watch the wind's movements through what it does. Be aware of what a mighty force it can be.

Realize the same air moves in your lungs. The wind and the air are precious to all life on earth.

## Prayer

Blessed are you, Holy Spirit of God, unseen yet ever present, the breath of life.
We remember in your presence all whose lives are going through a stormy time.
We pray for all who are short of breath and are fearful.
We pray for all attempting to harness the wind as a means of power and light.
Holy Spirit, fill us with your power and enlighten our lives with your love.
Blessed are you, Holy Spirit of God.

# WATER

# *Water*

Water is made up of two flammable gases, oxygen and hydrogen. When two hydrogen atoms combine with one larger oxygen atom, the hydrogen atoms hold tightly on to their host, but they also make casual bonds to other water molecules. The nature of water molecules seems like dancing the Dashing White Sergeant at high speed, briefly joining up with another threesome and then moving on in ever-changing partnerships, billions of times a second. At any given moment, only about 15 per cent of molecules are touching, which is why we can put our hand into water or swim in it.

Water is a miracle in itself. Many of its properties are unique and necessary to the existence of life upon the earth. Most substances contract with cold and expand with heat, and water is no exception – until it reaches 4 degrees centigrade. At this temperature, just above freezing point, it begins to expand as it cools, and as it turns into ice it expands even more. This process is essential for the life of the earth and is without parallel. If water and ice continued to contract as they cooled, the cool water would sink and ice would form at the bottom of the pond or the sea rather than at the top. At the top, it melts again as soon as there is a rise in temperature. At the bottom, it would not melt and would build up year after year until all was ice. This would make life on earth impossible.

Water plays an essential role in maintaining the temperature of the earth and the temperature of our bodies. It is uniquely suited to do this because of two of its properties. First, it absorbs a lot of heat. It takes a great deal of heat to raise its temperature – that's why it takes so long to boil a kettle of water. Second, water is thin. Compared with oil or treacle, water flows quickly and easily. This is important as it is the basis of our circulatory system. If water were thicker, the heart would have to work much harder. When it carries other cells, like blood cells, it flows even faster. You may find it interesting to know our bodies are made up of about 62 per cent water. A cow is 74 per cent water, a potato 80 per cent, a melon 92 per cent and a tomato is nearly all water at 95 per cent.

## The gift of water

Water, in all the universe,
there is nothing quite like you.
The miracle you have wrought
on our 'Blue Planet'!
You contribute to the harmony of the earth,
our wonderful position in the solar system
and our special place in the universe.
Through you we see the relationship
we share with everything in creation.
You are more than a wonderful gift
for without you we would not exist.
May we never take you for granted
or do you harm through pollution:
for it is not only the fish of the ocean,
the brown trout in the rivers,
the tadpoles in the pools

that need you
but all life on earth.
Let us treasure your existence
and give praise to your Creator.

## Exercise

Go out for a walk by the sea, a river or a lake. How often do you enjoy the presence of water? Do you realize what a miracle water is, how precious for life?

Give thanks for this wonderful gift.

## Prayer

Blessed are you, Lord God, for our life, for our nurture and
    preservation,
for all that sustains, renews and refreshes us.
As we look at the running wave, the flowing stream, the water
    from our taps,
may we praise you for this precious gift that delights the eye
    and is so vital to our well-being.
Blessed are you, Lord God, giver of all that there is in creation.

# Oceans

It is because our oceans cover roughly 70 per cent of the surface area of the earth that it appears to be blue from space and is often referred to as the 'Blue Planet'. Around 3.5 billion years ago the oceans already had as much water as they hold now. To have maintained this gift for so long is a wonder of our planet and is unique, as far as we know.

Earth is the only planet in the solar system that has liquid water on its surface, and scientific research has not discovered flowing water anywhere else in the universe. There is water vapour and ice to be found but not flowing water, as the other planets are either too close to the sun or too far away from it.

Water is necessary for life on earth, though nearly 97 per cent of the world's water is too salty for human use. The volume of our oceans is around 332.5 million cubic miles and, as a single cubic mile equals more than 1.1 trillion gallons, that is an awful lot of water! The Pacific Ocean holds over half all oceanic water at 51.6 per cent, the Atlantic holds 23.6 per cent and the Indian Ocean holds 21.2 per cent. This leaves just 3.6 per cent for all the other seas.

The oceans absorb great quantities of heat from the sun and transport it around the world by means of oceanic currents. This helps to keep earth's temperature relatively stable and uniform. In our bodies, water acts in much the same way. Water absorbs heat as it evaporates – more than any other fluid. So, as we sweat and the sweat evaporates, it has the effect of cooling our bodies down.

Of the 3 per cent of the world's water which is fresh, 90 per cent is in the Antarctica ice sheet, and most of the rest is in Greenland. The ice at the South Pole is 2 miles deep, whereas at the North Pole it is about 15 feet. The amount of water in rivers, lakes and reservoirs is only 0.036 per cent of all fresh water. Clouds and water vapour hold about 0.001 per cent.

## The water of life

It is no surprise that we are attracted to water.
Before we were born we swam in the waters of the womb:
our first world was a salty one
and so are our tears when, even now, we weep.
If we dehydrate we need a saline drip,
a fix of the ancient sea from where life forms began
(though the sea does have other salts
that our bodies can no longer tolerate).
More than half of the world's surface is water
and so are more than half of our bodies.
It is no surprise that we find watching it calming,
and entering it, embracing and enfolding.
Water has always been seen as a source of refreshment,
of healing, hydration and nourishment.
It is a delight to watch wave after wave
rolling in due to the pull of the tides
and the play of the wind:
to see the ocean crash against rocks with a mighty force,
or hear it roar as it pours over the breakwater,
mighty in power and beauty.

## Exercise

We call our planet 'earth' but in fact on the surface there is more water than earth. Look at the image of earth taken from space and see how blue it is due to air and water. Look at a map and see the vastness of the oceans. Yet even these great expanses are under threat. Try to think of ways that you can stop yourself adding to their pollution and give thanks for water in all its forms.

## Prayer

Blessed are you, Lord God, for the gift of water to the earth: for our mighty oceans and tiny streams, for rivers and lakes, and for the hydrological cycle that transports water around the world. Help us to remember that water is necessary for all life and teach us not to misuse or pollute it. Open our eyes to see that it is not only your gift but waits to reveal your glory to us. Blessed are you, Lord God, giver of water and life.

#  Rain

I went out to the car one cold morning and the inside of the windows were soon very wet. This happened because, as the car heated up, condensation formed on the cold glass: in other words, the water vapour in the air turned to liquid, to water. Rain originates in the same way. When atmospheric water vapour rises to form clouds, it meets colder air, condenses and forms water droplets. As these droplets come together and form heavier droplets then, due to gravity, they fall back to the earth as rain.

Clouds are not great reservoirs of water and hold only about 0.035 per cent of the earth's fresh water at any time. A fluffy summer cumulus would only fill a bath. When you walk 100 yards through a fog, you come in contact with only about a cubic inch of water, which is not even enough to fill a tea cup! Fog is cloud that lacks the power to fly.

Rain is precious to the earth, for without it plants would die and the land would become a desert. If you visit dry places on the earth, this is instantly apparent. We need the rains in their seasons to replenish our rivers, streams and reservoirs, to grow crops and maintain the life of grasses and trees.

Rain is something we take for granted. But we are in danger of interfering with its cycle through polluting the air. If we disturb the well-being of the earth upon which we live, we cannot hope to be healthy or at ease on this planet that is our home. Already around our world, people and nations are suffering from changes in climate that are often having violent and disastrous results. We need to heed the warning and read the signs of our times.

## Rain

I am watching heavy rainfall and thinking of how all things are linked.

The same dynamics that created time and space and shaped the universe are at work.

The gravity that caused the stars to shine causes the rain to fall.

The first waters on the earth, after it was sufficiently cooled, are still a mystery.

Did the earth itself give birth to the oceans or was water brought by meteors of ice hitting the earth during the Great Bombardment? It could easily have been both.

While the earth was full of volcanic action, there was no rain but it was enveloped by a great dust cloud which protected it from the sun's radiation.

It did not rain for millennia. And then it rained for hundreds of years with mighty storms and lightning like the world has not seen since, lightning being one of the factors in producing life. Again the mysterious source at work.

The first rains were so acidic no being could have survived in them.

The first life forms were microbes that in time learned photo-synthesis, changed the oxygen level in our atmosphere, and helped the rain to be as we know it now.

It is intriguing to think how many things are involved in the rain falling.

Rain, keeping me indoors, you are a wonderful gift, life giving and life renewing.
Each drop that falls holds the mystery that created the universe and is a wonder to behold.
I am going to have a walk in the rain.

## Exercise

Go for a walk in the rain, conscious that it is renewing the
soil, the plants, the trees, and replenishing our rivers. It is a
great gift and you are dependent on it. See if you can find
ways of discovering its wonderful power and give thanks.

## Prayer

Blessed are you, Lord God,
for the life-giving waters of the earth,
for the rains that bring refreshment to the dry land and
renewal to living things.
Teach us that we have a delicate and important relationship
with the rain
and guide us in ways to ensure that we do not disrupt this
balance.
Blessed are you, Lord God, who gives us the waters of life.

#  Rivers

High in the mountains and hills, rain or melting snow forms into rivulets and descends as streams. These join up with other tributaries, which add to their volume, and they become rivers. Rivers are dynamic things, forever changing their shape and the land over which they travel, tumbling over rocks, creating waterfalls . . . As they leave the mountains, however, rivers slow down, seek the path of least resistance and finally flow into a lake or ocean. Where the river is muddy and the land flat, the sediments it lays down, including minerals and rich nutrients from plants and animals, may form a delta. The place where a river meets the tide is one of the most biologically productive parts of all. Most of the world's fish catch comes from species that are dependent for at least part of their life cycle on a nutrient-rich estuarine habitat.

It was natural for humans to seek to live by water. Evidence of our change from nomadic hunters and gathers to farmers was found in the narrow river valleys of the mountains of the Near East, at archaeological sites between 9,000 and 10,000 years old. The first civilizations emerged in the third millennium BC along the Euphrates, the Tigris, the Nile and the Indus, and some time after along the Yellow River in China. Much later, during the Industrial Revolution, new towns grew up along the rivers and streams which powered the early industrial factories.

Rivers are not only full of life but contribute to our lives. As well as being a joy to be beside, they have acted over the centuries as waterways for the movement of people and goods. However, we have misused them too. In the 1960s, the world began to realize it was poisoning its rivers with too much human and factory waste. Fish were dying or leaving never to return. Some rivers were too toxic and dangerous to swim in. Fertilizers from farming were making some streams clog up with growth. Over the last 50 years, there have been great efforts to clean up our rivers. Fish have returned or been reintroduced and our rivers are much healthier than they have been for a long time.

## A small stream

The Waren Burn, which has its source a few miles from my home in the hills near Warenton, is not big enough to be called a river.

It has had its name since the Celtic tribes lived in the area and used its resources, but there have been people living near the burn since the last ice age, as far back as we can trace.

Trees grow along the banks of the burn; a chestnut has flourished in the last few years, and alder and willow are very common.

I have watched the speckled trout and the wriggling eel and caught the heron fishing! I see frogs and moles. There is an abundance of birds, including the kingfisher, grey wagtail, dipper and, lately, egrets. The burn abounds with life and sustains life.

Where it pours into the sea at Budle Bay, wintering geese and waders gather in their thousands. Here the sediments brought down from the hill have enriched the Bay as a source of food.

The burn has sustained people, creatures and plants for thousands of years. It is believed there was a mill working by it in Saxon times.

I am grateful for rivers and streams, for the rain that refreshes and restores them, and for the mysterious presence they reveal.

I am ready to go out now and look at what is on and in the burn today: it is part of my daily routine.

## Exercise

Go for a walk by your nearest river and discover what kind of life and communities it supports. If it is a small river, you might like to trace it to its source. Rest by it and enjoy it. Give thanks for the water of life.

## Prayer

Lord God who created the great deeps, we thank you
for the rains that water the earth,
for sparkling burns and running streams,
for mighty rivers and reservoirs,
for the clear water supply in our homes.
We remember in your presence those who lack good water,
those who have to walk a long way to fetch it,
those who live in areas of drought,
and those whose water is badly polluted.
We ask your blessing upon all who are seeking
to provide good water for everyone.

# EARTH

# 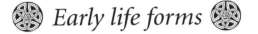 Early life forms

No one is sure how the miracle of life began. Life's building blocks are really nothing more than an intricate and ordered system of simple and complex molecules. However, the chances that these building blocks could just decide to form life is zero. There is mystery involved.

We have discovered that life could have begun in the depths of the ocean through the production of the right elements around the energy source of the volcanic vents, or by pools of the right materials being struck by lightning at the edge of the tides. Some have suggested it may have been brought to earth by meteorites of ice.

More than 3.5 billion years ago, when the earth was young and turbulent and suffering great lightning storms, the earliest life forms appeared in the shape of tiny microbes which have been named prokaryotes and reproduced by splitting themselves in half. Some people believe it is possible that some of these earliest microbes are still alive today!

The next amazing event is that one or several families of these microbes not only developed the power of sexual reproduction but passed that power on to the next generation in the beginning of DNA. Throughout the early ages they reproduced themselves and fed on the energy-rich turbulent hot earth. During this time, they mutated and changed through their relationships with each other.

All life began with microbes and still depends on them: they are one of the most successful and innovative creatures in existence. They began to fill the earth and, after maybe a billion years, one of these families, Oceanic cyanobacteria, which had its home in the seas, discovered how to use photosynthesis and a new age dawned.

## A cautionary tale

The early earth was carbon- and hydrogen-rich, and the cyanobacteria took the hydrogen from the sea and released oxygen into the air. As the first free oxygen was released through photosynthesis, it was initially soaked up by iron dissolved in the oceans and formed red-coloured iron oxide, which settled to the ocean floor. Over time, distinctive sedimentary rocks called banded iron formations were created by these iron oxide deposits. About 2.4 billion years ago, when the iron in the oceans was used up, oxygen started building up in the atmosphere.

The metabolic process of these tiny microorganisms as they grew in number increased the oxygen in the air to about its present 21 per cent of the atmosphere. This set the earth's original atmosphere off balance, as the rising oxygen level was toxic to many of the early microbiotic creatures and may have destroyed most living organisms at the time. Cyanobacteria were therefore responsible for one of the most significant extinction events in the earth's history.

If cyanobacteria had continued increasing in great numbers, the atmosphere would have become so oxygen-rich, the world would have ended up in flames. But the cyanobacteria found the oxygen-rich atmosphere poisonous to their own genetic structure, so they went deeper to the bottom of lakes or hid inside other creatures that were able to survive the higher level of oxygen. It was these new oxygen-tolerant creatures that would now develop, and in their use of oxygen help to keep it at the present level.

We live in a wonderful world of checks and balances. Give thanks for cyanobacteria that prepared the earth for us. But heed this warning of this story!

## Exercise

You may have traced your family tree but have you ever thought that in the far distant past one of your ancestors was a superstar? And if that makes you feel proud, that another was a microbe? You share your beginning with the plants and early creatures. If this chain of being had been broken you would not exist. Spend some time giving thanks for your own unique life and the very fact that you are here at all.

## Prayer

Creator of all, let us be aware of the mysterious web of life,
and how each creature is a part of that web, and all are
    precious.
You have created a wonderful diversity of species and indi-
    viduals within each species, and all are unique.
No two flowers are the same, no two fish, no two birds, no
    two mammals . . .
May we seek to protect and show respect for every part of
    your creation and to discover each is a manifestation
    of creativity and love.

#  Soil

Tread gently on the soil, for you tread on that on which your life depends. Soil is made up of living and non-living materials, normally about 45 per cent minerals, 25 per cent water, 25 per cent air and 5 per cent organic matter from decaying plants and animals.

In many parts of Britain, it is only around 10,000 years since the last ice age stripped away the surface soils. It takes about 500 years to produce an inch of topsoil which is the most productive layer. The minerals in the soil come from rocks broken down mainly by water, wind and time. The organic matter, often called 'humus', is the most important part: it has been estimated that there are more microorganisms in a good handful of soil than there are people on earth. Due to the organic matter, all sorts of reactions are going on in the water and air space of the soil. Seen under a microscope, it teems with life. The roots of trees and tunnelling creatures, such as worms, turn the soil over and help to break it down. Soil is at the bottom of the food chain, but it is the cornerstone of life on earth.

We need to be aware that much of the soil of our planet is endangered by human expansion: indeed, an area the size of Wales is lost every ten years. As cities have grown up, with their new roads, housing estates and other developments, topsoil has often been dug up and dumped as if it were of no value, or it is covered over with concrete.

It is too easy to take the productivity of our soil for granted. In many areas, it is being overworked by a constant use of chemicals. Bad land-management practices, overgrazing, pollution and deforestation are all causing degradation and threatening the capability of the land to meet the needs of future generations. For healthy communities we need healthy soil and a healthy earth. If soil is poor, people will be poor too.

## Dear friend

You have always been with me,
yet I have failed to love you;
I have treated you like dirt,
yet you have nourished me.
In warm days l lay upon you
and smelt your earthiness.
Other times I have ignored you,
yet still you care for me.
I have trodden upon you,
jumped up and down on you,
yet you faithfully serve me.
When they stripped you,
I admired your shape,
your wonderful symmetry.
Then I overworked you,
pouring chemicals upon you.
But still, you provide for me.
I have treated you like rubbish,
I have poisoned you,
and you still feed me.

May I learn to care for you
as you always care for me.
For in you is life
and without you I would die.

## Exercise

Look over a park or an open field and consider the millions of living creatures working to keep the underlying soil healthy. Think how soil is the base line for nearly all of life. If you have a garden, you may consider what chemicals, if any, you use. You could also help your soil by giving it some attention – and some new compost!

## Prayer

Blessed are you, Lord God, who made the earth,
who raised up the mountains and shaped the dry land.
You created the rivers and formed the soils,
giving us a fertile and beautiful earth.
We give you thanks for the gift of soil,
praying we may respect and care for this precious thing
with a sense of awe and wonder.
Let us tread gently on the earth,
live to care for your creation
and glorify your holy name.

 *Trees*

Plants were the first life form to venture out of the sea. They arrived into a bare landscape, with no greenery, no living soil, only mile upon mile of baked rocks and rubble. How many died at the high-tide mark of the sea before some took root? We will never know. Around 360 million years ago, the first wood cells came into being in damp areas. They were lycopods, club mosses and giant horsetails. Prolific in their growth, in dying these plants laid down many of the rich coalfields of the world. But they needed a wet world in which to live and reproduce.

Then around 350 million years ago, there was an important step forward. The first conifers developed a strong vascular system and put down roots in the rubble and rock. They had naked seeds that did not require a damp atmosphere. The gingko, dawn redwood and monkey puzzle tree belong to this period of time and have changed very little since.

Around 150 million years ago came the first broadleaved trees. With their powers of photosynthesis, they absorbed carbon dioxide from the air and breathed out oxygen, utilizing the power of the sun. Their roots burrowed down through rocky surfaces. Dead wood leads to the formation of complex soils, and the soil's humus is by and large the polymer that makes wood tough.

Ninety-five million years ago, a new age of hardwoods began. The oak, sycamore, maple, magnolia and laurel all proliferated and began to dominate. However, by the end of the Devonian era, trees had consumed so much carbon dioxide that the air cooled dramatically. This led to the creation of the ice cap at the South Pole and the demise of a huge number of unique animals and plants all over the earth. Yet trees were actually leading the way for a new stage in the world.

## A woodland walk

I walked into the autumn wood,
to ease my restless mind:
seeking shelter from the wind
among the sunlit dappled trees –
gold, lime green, a touch of red,
a brown crisp carpet on the ground;
beech masts, acorns, hazelnut,
now hidden and carefully covered,
but yet such miracles to see.
I have not given anything to you,
but your gifts to me are boundless,
and such beauty calms my mind.
While you enrich with trunk, and leaf,
your every breath blesses the air.
The world would be lost without you.
An ancient onlooker, standing strange,
silently and strong, was the mighty
monkey puzzle tree.
Its ancestors made these trees
one by one in creation's progression
over the millennia, through mayhem
in stately slow and strict succession.

Deeply blessed and rested,
I walked out of the autumn wood.

## Exercise

Go and walk in the woods for the sheer joy of being there. Look at the light through the trees, admire them and seek to see them for the miracle that they are. There is no need to name each tree, yet some naming helps us to notice the wonderful variety there.

## Prayer

Blessed are you, Lord God of all creation.
In the woods and forests, you reveal the rich connectedness
   of all your creation.
May we learn to respect and to care for your forests, the lungs
   of the earth,
and for all indigenous forest-dwellers, human and animal.
Blessed are you, Lord God of all creation.

# 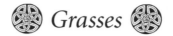 *Grasses*

All grasses, plants and flowers descend from the earliest trees. By dropping their leaves and eventually rotting, trees enriched the soil and prepared the way for new plants – and for land creatures. Among the first were the millipedes. A millipede fossil, found in some of the oldest rocks in the world in Scotland, is the earliest creature we know of.

Grasses first appeared in the Cenozoic Era around 60 million years ago but large grasslands only date from 30 million years ago. With them came numerous rodents, which were for a while the main herbivore. Soon to follow were larger mammals, as the grassland covered the continents.

Most of the time we take grass for granted but it is important to life. Grasslands cover 20 per cent of all land on earth, with over 10,000 species found in vast prairies, savannahs and steppes – from the baking equator to the Arctic Circle. Grasses include the great Dragon Bamboos of South Asia, as well as rice, maize and wheat, and the lawns of our homes and parks.

Unlike other plants, grasses grow from their base rather than their tip, so they are almost indestructible, capable of surviving fire, flood, frost and drought, grazing by animals and mowing by humans. Grasslands support and sustain more large animals than any other habitat and are home to the greatest gatherings of wildlife on earth. Let us remember that this includes us.

**Lament for a hay meadow**

The year the farmer ploughed the hay meadow
I felt bereft; it had been there since my birth.
Machinery had done its work
and the creatures had lost their home.
Sweet grasses, corn cockle and bunting,
the lark song from the sky,
the yellow buttercup and the bees,
all disappeared without time for goodbye.
The lady's mantle and her bedstraw,
the oxeye daisies and the camomile,
never to be seen here any more.
To lose flowers, birds and creatures
feels like a total eclipse of the sun.

**Exercise**

If you are able, go and look at a meadow in the spring or
summer. See what wild life abounds, listen to the bird sounds,
smell the air. Can you distinguish between bales of hay and
straw? Do you know the difference between hay and silage?
Failing a visit, see if you can find paintings or photographs of
hay meadows and admire their beauty.

**Prayer**

Blessed are you, Lord Creator, and lover of all.
You have given us the grasses of the earth to nourish us
and provide our daily bread.
Teach us to respect the grasses, without which we would die.
We cannot create grass but only work in cooperation with it.

So many creatures are endangered by our misuse of our
   powers.
Lord, save us from plundering the world to satisfy our own
   ends alone.
Teach us that we belong to this wonderful and intricate web
   of life,
and to harm a strand within it is to harm ourselves.
Blessed are you, Lord Creator, and lover of all.

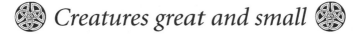# Creatures great and small

If you imagine the earth's history portrayed in a single day it would look something like this:

**4.00 a.m.**    Origin of life.

**2.08 p.m.**    Single-celled algae.
In the next few hours, there are major steps forward: sexual reproduction, and the use of photosynthesis, necessary for life as we know it.

**8.30 p.m.**    The first multicellular animals, sea plants, seaweeds.

**8.50 p.m.**    Jellyfish, sea pens and flat worms in the oceans.

**9.04 p.m.**    Trilobites, sea snails and clams are soon followed by vertebrate animals, some of which develop jaws and fins.

**9.52 p.m.**    The first trees, lycopods, develop the wood cell. Soon after, crawling then flying insects, Later, vertebrates go ashore; amphibians.

**10.45 p.m.**    The first land-worthy seeds by conifers and the growth of the carboniferous forests which lay down great coal seams. Reptiles with land-worthy eggs, and warm-blooded reptiles. Then the Permian extinctions when 75 to 95 per cent of all species are eliminated.

| | |
|---|---|
| **10.56 p.m.** | Dinosaurs, flowering plants spread and the insects that feed off them. |
| **11.39 p.m.** | The first mammals, birds, marsupials, placental animals and primates. The land and seas teem with life. The first placental mammals appear 114 million years ago and give birth to live young. Cretaceous extinction happened around 67 million years ago. |

The Cenozoic Era was one of amazing creativity 55 million years ago. Early forms of whales, horses, bats, rodents and monkeys.

By 40 million years ago, various orders of mammals complete; 37 million years ago, the earth suffered from a cosmic impact. As the world recovers, early cats, dogs and monkeys. Around 30 million years ago, the first apes, and 25 million years ago whales become the largest animal in the sea of all time.

| | |
|---|---|
| **11.51 p.m.** | In a warmer climate, grasses grow and early antelopes appear. Cosmic impact: the Miocene catastrophe. As life recovers, a surge in grazing animals: gibbons, orang-utans, gorillas, modern cats and dogs and elephants appear. Then 5 million years ago, chimpanzees and hominids come on to the scene. Next would come camels, bears, pigs, horses and cattle. |
| **11.58 and 43 seconds p.m.** | Around 2.6 million years ago, the first humans, *Homo habilis*, using stone tools. A new era for the world. |

## Life is precious

All life is precious and all comes from the same Originating Power.

At the moment we know of nowhere else in the universe where there is life.

It is a wonderful gift to the earth.

It has taken four billion years of creativity, disaster, newness of life through genetic mutation, natural selection and conscious choice for us to live. Stop and give thanks for all of life.

We see time and again through global history how fragile life is, yet how resilient it appears to be. We discover how health depends on the earth, the air, the temperature, the water. What changes the climate affects everything. Dwell for a while on the ways we are now endangering the future of humankind if not all life on earth.

Over 4 billion years, what we have designated as five kingdoms have come into being. The first is that of bacteria, the oldest, most prolific and hardiest form of life. There are more bacteria in your stomach than people on the earth. Nothing can live without bacteria.

The next kingdom is that of eukaryotic cells, with over 65,000 species identified. They are the basis of all life, including the third, fourth and fifth kingdoms of fungi, plants and animals.

We would have no existence without eukaryotic cells, or the various sea creatures that developed vertebrae, lungs, jaws and eyes. We needed trees to prepare the earth for life, amphibians to come ashore, insects to fertilize flowers, grasses for grazing animals. Spend time appreciating how we are part of a very intricate web of life.

## Exercise

Realize what an amazing being you are. The odds of you ever existing would be rated at zero. Without the Creative Source you would not exist. Without the right balance of the universe you would not have any being. Without the primary elements' power to create there would be no creation. Without the whole procession of beings, you would never have arrived.

Your family tree includes the Originating Source, stars and superstars as well as bacteria!

Rejoice in the wonder of life, the diversity of creation and your own being.

## Prayer

Blessed are you, Creator of all:
**I praise your mighty power.**
For sun and moon and shining stars,
for wind and rain and snow,
for seas and rivers and all that live within them:
**I praise your mighty power.**
For mountains and hills and valleys,
for trees and flowers and grasses and all that grows in the
    ground,
for wild animals and creeping things and flying birds:
**I praise your mighty power.**

For all that has led up to my being alive,
for the web of life of which I am part,
for my loved ones, friends and neighbours:
**I praise your mighty power.**

# HUMANKIND

#  *Stages*

To understand our family tree, we need to go back to the end of the Cretaceous period, around 65 to 55 million years ago, when primates came into being. This was a time of massive volcanic eruptions, and the earth suffered from the impact of a huge asteroid or comet that struck the seabed near the Yucatan Peninsula in Mexico. It has been suggested that its impact would have triggered a nuclear winter, and as the earth cooled and sea levels fell, dinosaurs, pterosaurs, several families of birds and mammals, marine animals, such as the plesiosaurs and ammonites, and many flowering plants would have been drastically affected. Some groups had been in decline for several million years before the final event that destroyed them. Up to 85 per cent of all species were lost, reminding us how fragile life on earth is.

The Cenozoic Era followed. Monkeys appeared around 36 million and apes around 30 million years ago. By 20 million years ago, monkeys and apes had split. In the development leading to hominids, gibbons, gorillas and the chimpanzee became separate species. Then around 5 million years ago, the first hominids appeared: they were distinguished by their larger brain size, their capacity for walking in an upright manner and their lack of tail. Although they still spent time in the trees, they mainly lived on the great grass plains that had formed.

At this stage in our development, 4 million years ago, a young hominid, thought to be female, lived in southern

Ethiopia. She has been given the name Lucy and, like other hominids, appears to have been vegetarian. Two such hominids, walking erect, left 60 footprints in some volcanic ash in northern Tanzania. Other hominid remains had been found earlier and many more have been found since.

## Meditating on evolution

Evolution is not automatic, it is affected by chance and choice. When a living creature's circumstances alter, the creature must choose to change or it will not survive. This is what shapes much of life of earth. It is awesome that the universe is not only created but creative. It shares these powers with the Originating Source. All of life on earth is an ongoing drama of intelligent choice. Sometimes change comes about unexpectedly through a genetic mutation. Though uncommon, this may occur once in about every 100,000 replications, and be passed on in a newly formed sequence of material in the DNA of the species. Sometimes this leads to a group or species simply not surviving. There is an element of wildness that we can neither understand nor control. It is a miracle we are here.

Changes in climate and the growth of the savannahs encouraged our ancestors to cease being tree-dwellers and to walk upright on the great plains of the earth.

As mentioned above, the physical changes that led to the separate identity of humans are an increase in the cranium vault to hold a larger brain size, bipedal walking, which altered leg formation, and the development of the spinal column through upright posture. Upright posture puts demands on the pelvis, as it has to bear the load of the body and whatever is carried. To strengthen the pelvis, the birth canal in the female has to be comparatively narrow. This has two effects: birthing is painful and poses danger to mother and child, and at birth a child is small and helpless, necessitating strong family bonding of male and female.

Other physical changes include the frontal focus of eyes and face, the development of hands for grasping and the working of the hands and arms in relationship to the eye. The upright posture freed the hands to carry things and later to shape all sorts of tools and useful items. The immediate consequence of using the hands was to free the jaw from having to carry and hold on to objects: this led to a refinement of the face, the throat, the tongue, the cheeks and lips, which would later be used in the development of speech.

We should be grateful for all of this as it led to our being.

### Exercise

Give thanks for the dexterity that humans have acquired, for our ability to walk upright, to run and to be still. Give thanks for the power of speech and the ability to communicate. Rejoice in the wonder of your being and in life itself.

### Prayer

Blessed are you, Lord God of all creation,
to you be praise and glory for ever.
From the beginning you have created all things,
bestowing life on the creatures of the earth.
In time you created us, giving us breath and speech,
dexterity in movement and amazing abilities.
May we use these gifts to your praise and glory.
Blessed are you, Lord God, now and for ever.

# 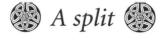 A split

In the beginning, hominids were in a world where most creatures were stronger than they were, many animals were faster, toothier and more ferocious. In the savannahs, hominids would hardly be noticed by any other creature as they gathered food. This first transition towards humankind is best documented in Kenya, Tanzania and Ethiopia.

The earliest humans show an increase in brain size. Around 2.6 million years ago a species transition took place and a new mode of activity appeared, with the making of tools and later with the control of fire. Along with this we see a development in physical and social activity. These humans were more refined in feature, with smaller teeth than their predecessors and more competent in their interactions with the environment. They have been given the name *Homo habilis*, meaning the toolmaker. *Homo habilis* worked in the region of Olduvai in the Great Rift Valley of Kenya, where he made tools from river pebbles including flint: these were created not only to be used but to be beautiful. There was such an abundance it is thought a primitive factory might have existed, with tools used to trade for other things. This would demonstrate a developed sense of social relationship and the forming of community. Tools would be used for the killing of animals and smaller versions for dissecting the kill. No longer was *Homo habilis* a gatherer: he had become a hunter and meat-eater too.

The next phase began with another increase in brain size around 1.5 million years ago. *Homo erectus* were the first we know of to migrate out of Africa, initially through the Asian world, then through southern and western Europe. They were known as Trinil humans in Java and Sinanthropus in China. As hunter-gatherers they lived in semi-permanent encampments and were still relatively small groups, erecting shelters or using caves for their dwellings.

## Meditation on hunter-gatherers

It takes a keen eye, a sure hand and an idea of what you want to produce a flint instrument. I have some in my possession: flint arrow heads, spears and an axe made from what looks like a river pebble. I remember the joy of finding the axe head. It had been buried under a layer of soil and a rabbit burrowing had uncovered it. All my implements could still be used today for the purposes for which they were manufactured. Some look as if they were made for their sheer beauty; they are masterpieces that demonstrate the skill of their creator.

Think of a group of craftsmen, sitting by the edge of a lake or river, foraging to find materials, planning the production of useful instruments. Did they ever take orders? What would be used in trade? Was much of the work done by an extended family or by a close yet small tribal group? Their place of work has been described as a 'factory' and a 'shop': were apprentices taken on to learn the trade? If the craftsmen – or perhaps craftswomen? – spent a lot of time working on making tools, were they dependent on others to hunt for food?

Making weapons would give these early humans a sense of power. They were moving from being gatherers to hunters, vegetarians to meat-eaters. Hunting changed their lifestyle and must have done something to their psyche for they now had in their hands the power of life and death. From this beginning, humankind would continue to build ever more efficient weapons until today, when we have the power to destroy all life on earth. Real progress is intrinsically bound up with wisdom and sensibility, which *Homo sapiens* does not always possess.

## Exercise

Think of all the people on whom you are dependent for your food: farmers and fishermen and -women, market gardeners, millers and butchers, dairy workers, transporters and those who work in shops. Be grateful for their labour and, where possible, thank them personally for what they do.

## Prayer

Blessed are you, Lord our Creator:
you gave us eyes to see,
mouths so we can speak,
hands to hold, and to use in creating,
ears to attend to the voices of the earth,
hearts to be open to love and to love,
lives to share and to show our care.
Blessed are you, Lord our Creator.

# 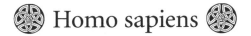 Homo sapiens

Two hundred thousand years ago a more intelligent, capable and lither species appeared, to which we have given the name *Homo sapiens*. These people are the ancestors of all humans alive today. It is thought they came out of the African plains and migrated in time as far afield as the Americas and Australia, adapting to varying climates and geographical terrain.

*Homo sapiens* went through two main phases, the archaic and the modern. The archaic phase, as it existed in Europe, is associated with the Middle Palaeolithic period from 120,000 to 4,000 years ago. The remains of such people were found in the Neander Valley in Germany and they were given the name Neandertal. They were more physically robust, with a larger brain capacity and heavier and more protruding features than modern humans. They lived in caves, used fire, wore personal ornaments and used flint tools.

The world was going through climate change when modern *Homo sapiens* appeared in Europe. The last great ice age affected the biosystems of the earth, with trees, plants and animals moving south in order to survive. It was as the ice retreated that the Cro-Magnon people appeared. They were more creative, inventive and artistic than their predecessors: their paintings and many sculptures have been found in over 200 caves. They used lamps, with fuel coming from animal fat, and also had a range of cooking utensils and a variety of containers made of pottery and of wood. Some of their hunting weapons were decorated with naturalistic patterns. It is apparent that they had some knowledge of tailoring from the existence of a small sculpted figure from Russia dating from 20,000 years ago, and from a fully clothed man of the same period, who was buried near Moscow. His garment has decayed but the beads that remain indicate how artistic its makers were. Although modern *Homo sapiens* dwelt in caves where available, they also lived in extensive habitations of pits dug into the earth, paved with smooth stones, with a canopy of skin or plant covering over timbers. It would take until around 8000 BC before such small encampments became villages. Between 8000 BC and 3000 BC, village life was based on horticulture and the domestication of animals, and this agricultural basis was of prime importance. Large communities grew around places where water was plentiful; Jericho, for example, had around 3,000 inhabitants.

And, as they say, 'the rest is history'.

## Meditation on cave paintings

Deep in the places where cave paintings originated, artists would require light to see and to work with. They would need a range of colouring material, something to contain these in, and implements for applying them. Some paintings are situated in places that would have required a form of ladder or scaffolding. Then there had to be an idea of what the artist would paint. Capturing shape and beauty demands a good eye and hand, a honed memory and a sensitivity to the subject of the painting (animal figures being by far the most common). Sometimes there would be agreement to work with others, which would take planning and cooperation and, obviously, the ability to communicate in speech.

In this relating to certain animals and to each other, we see an early expression of the human psyche. And if you enter a cave to view the art by a flickering flame, you may sense the sacredness of a special place. Did some of these creatures have a mythical quality about them, or did the people recognize all life as sacred? These wonderfully creative expressions reveal a capacity for more than just thought, with emotion if not devotion displayed. How far the brain, the eye and the hand have come over the ages. But how much have we really advanced since then?

## Exercise

As artists, poets and musicians all try to help us perceive a deeper reality in the world around us, look at a copy of one of the cave paintings, preferably by candlelight in a darkened room. Gaze at it and let it show you the depth and mystery of life. You could do the same with a painting or a photograph of a hare, a deer or any other creature. Afterwards try to visu alize what you have been looking at and see how much of its essence you can capture on paper in art or words.

## Prayer

Creator God, we give you thanks and praise,
for you have allowed us to share in your creative powers
and to bring many new inventions and creations into being.
We give you thanks for all scientists and inventors,
for artists, sculptors and musicians, for poets, writers and
    actors,

for architects, planners and builders.
We give you thanks for all who encourage us to look outwards,
beyond ourselves, and to be aware of the mysteries and wonders of creation.
Blessed are you, Lord God of all creation.

# ✿ The dangerous animal ✿

Some believe the human race is out of control and heading for disaster. The population has, until recently, grown very slowly: diseases kept life expectancy short and death rates high in pre-industrial society. It took until 1804 for the human population to reach its first billion, and another 123 years to reach 2 billion. In 1960 it had reached 3 billion, and in just under 40 years it had doubled to 6 billion. The present world population is 7.3 billion and rising rapidly, diminishing the earth's finite resources, such as fossil fuels and minerals. As a result, pollution is on the rise.

To cope with the increase in population, most farms have been encouraged to deep plough with heavy machinery, which impacts the earth, and to use insecticides and fertilizers. There is a danger these things will kill off the natural fertility of the soil. If the land is not healthy, we cannot remain healthy for long. Over the last 30 years the insect population of the earth has plummeted by three-quarters. You may say, 'So what?!' But insects are necessary for pollinating and so ensuring that plants reproduce. Insects account for two-thirds of life on earth and are indicative of a healthy planet. To lose them would be catastrophic. Maurice Maeterlinck said, 'If the bee disappears from the face of the earth man would only have four years to live.'[1]

The seas are faring no better than the land. Excessive fishing has depleted stocks, not only for humans but sea birds and other creatures that depend on them. The sea is so polluted with plastic that most fish are absorbing some. Even seven miles down, in the deepest part of the ocean in the Mariana Trench, sea creatures are eating plastic. It also threatens whales and dolphins as they ingest it. Each year about 320 million tons of plastic is produced globally. How much more can the sea absorb before there is a point of no return?

The air that is a necessity to all life is also under threat. Even now the pollution from diesel fuel is making our cities unhealthy places to live in. Worse still, we are affecting the earth's carbon cycle. The earth has been naturally processing 2 billion tons of carbon a year in wonderfully graceful ways. But we are recklessly adding a further 6 billion and causing changes that are already having disastrous effects on our atmosphere.

Humans are a danger to themselves and to the whole of earth. It is not progress to take what we want without regard for the result. We must consider what is good for the world, for if the world is impoverished we cannot be rich. Every time a creature is lost, something is lost in us. Every time we pollute the air, we are risking the very existence of life.

## Meditation on listening to the world

Yet, there is still hope. Already some changes have been made. The year 2017 was the first year that Britain produced more power from renewable resources than from fossil fuels, which meant putting less carbon into the atmosphere. Around the world, many areas are now protected against over-fishing, and in such places fish are increasing in number. A lot of work is being done to protect endangered species. There are plans to phase out the use of diesel fuel in cars.

We are moving away from the idea that the earth is ours to use as we like. We have the ability to change, and if countries are willing to cooperate we can soon begin to make a difference.

We must learn to cooperate with the earth's processes and to yield to its limits. Even more importantly, we must learn to acknowledge that creation is full of mystery and we will never entirely understand it. But we can certainly direct more resources into solving earth's problems. Of course, vested interests, human greed and the capacity to act like naughty children trashing our home may hinder us.

We must abandon arrogance and stand in awe. We must recover a sense of the majesty of creation and adore in the presence of its maker. For I do not doubt that it is only through reverence for the world that our species will be able to remain in it. Let us learn to listen to what the air, the seas, the land and the creatures are telling us and act together to protect and renew the wonderful web of life on earth.

## Exercise

My hope is that you love the world and respect its fragility and its life forms. Check that you are concerned about what is happening to land, sea and air. Look at each and see how you can help to show your care. Make considered decisions about what you can do. Perhaps compile a list of changes you personally could undertake.

**Prayer**

God our Creator, who created the world out of love and for
    love,

help us to respect the intricate and fragile web of your
    creation.

In a world of great variety of creatures, may we respect and
    care for all.

Help us to stop polluting our land or overworking it.

May we learn how to cleanse our air and to stop overload-
    ing it.

Teach us to respect all sources of water and not to use them
    as rubbish dumps.

May we learn to reverence the great forests that sustain much
    life and cleanse our air.

Teach us to love the world with the love that you have for the
    world.

# CONCLUSION

#  *Wonder*

This has been quite a speedy journey from the beginning of creation until now! You may ask, 'What is the reason for it?' My hope is that it has opened your eyes and your heart to the wonder of all creation and to its source out of No-thing. For me it has been an act of wonder, love and praise. Who can grasp that at the beginning we came from No-thing? It is beyond the limits of our comprehension. It is awesome to look at hydrogen and see that as a 'layer is peeled off' – rather like a Russian doll – something new is revealed. We have learned that single-celled bacteria are anything but simple, and that multicelled bacteria prepared the earth for the diversity of life. In the coming forth of sea creatures, then land and air creatures, there is marvel upon marvel. If we can look at this unfolding without wonder and love, we have lost a precious part of our being. Wonder and love are gifts that we are born with but often they are not awakened or have atrophied from lack of use. One of the greatest needs in education is to develop these gifts in our offspring before we ever begin to cram them with knowledge. Children are not vessels to be filled as much as lamps to be lit: they already have deep within them gifts beyond description, wholly worthy of being sought out. I am fully in agreement with Einstein when he said:

Whoever is devoid of the capacity of wonder, whoever remains unmoved, whoever cannot contemplate or know the deep shudder of the soul in enchantment, might just as well be dead for he has already closed his eyes upon life.[1]

And with St Paul writing to the Corinthians when he said:

If I speak with the tongues of mortals and of angels, but do not have love, I am a noisy gong or a clanging cymbal. And if have prophetic powers, and understand all mysteries and all knowledge, and if I have all faith, so as to remove mountains, but do not have love, I am nothing.[2]

However, our familiarity with the world, and the orderliness and ordinariness of our daily routines, tends to dull the senses and hide the wonder of our being here at all. We crowd our lives with agendas and activities, and our minds are so full of plans and pursuits that we rarely stop. For much of the day we are distracted and often distressed and seek to escape from these states by yet more activity. In doing so we become impoverished, no matter what we are earning or learning, for we are disconnected from any true relationship with the world, and even from our own inner being. Emptiness makes us crave excitement, possessions, anything for relief. Yet no matter what we do, that void in our lives will keep appearing.

Because we have lost any sense of wonder for the world, we are able to use it in harmful ways, to pollute it, destroy great parts of it, and ignore what our actions are doing. But there will be a day of awakening, for we cannot be healthy if the world in which we live is not a healthy place. If we create an environment not fit to live in, we will be responsible not only for our own demise but for that of many others. We need to recognize we are not separate from the world in which we live, and to be attentive in all we do.

The doorway to wonder and love is learning to be attentive, to live in the now: to be open to the present and beyond that the presence of the other before you. In fully attending to someone or something, we are giving them the greatest gift we have, which is our self.

There is great need in this age of 'selfies' for people who are not too wrapped up in their own ego. For this reason, I enjoy reading again and again the following words written by D. H. Lawrence:

> The only question to ask today, about a man or a woman,
> is: Has she chipped the shell of her own ego?
> Has he chipped the shell of his own ego?
> They are all perambulating eggs
> going: 'Squeak! Squeak! I am all things to myself,
> yet I can't be alone. I want somebody to keep me warm.'[3]

A lovely description of attentiveness: chipping the shell of your own ego. To help people come out of their protective shell and be open to what is round about, I have urged them to meditate on a single thing for about 20 minutes, and every time the mind wanders, to draw it back to the chosen subject. We should stay long enough with something to let it speak to us. Here briefly is what I have taught.

**Relax** and find yourself a comfortable place to sit or stand. Check your whole body, head to toe (or vice versa), and see that it is relaxed. Sometimes I suggest screwing up the face, clenching the hands tight and scrunching up the toes and then letting go. It's proof that you can relax your body!

**Be still** and watch your breathing. Breathe slowly and deeply with a gentle rhythm. You may like to close your eyes for a while when you do this.

Now **open your eyes** and focus on what you want to give yourself to: offer it your full attention. You may have chosen a tree, a flower, a leaf, a photograph, or a single word. Look at it with the eyes of your heart. Stop your thoughts from wandering and keep focused. Do not let preconceived ideas interfere with your relationship. Wait until the barriers fall and you see in front of you a subject in its own right. Let it communicate to you, know that it holds the mystery of all creation.

Before you leave, **acknowledge your subject** and give thanks for its being and the mystery it contains.

Once you have practised this for a while, use it to help you give your full attention to the people you are with and to any individual who comes to you. All are bearers of mysteries beyond our description but we may catch a sense of them.

We often fail to get to the reality that is about us, for we have not looked deep enough for long enough. Join me on a journey to be more open, to enter into a wonder-full world. I hope on this journey you will discover that:

1 every single thing is unique and full of wonder upon wonder;
2 each thing is a subject in its own right;
3 everything within creation has a potential to reveal deep mysteries;

4 you are steeped in that mystery and it is within you;

5 we are explorers of a world without frontiers;

6 every single moment is in eternity.

If you practise this each day you will make discoveries that help you enjoy the newness of life and the wonders it holds.

Sadly, much of our education segregates subjects as if they were independent of other subjects and spends a lot of time just giving us information. By means of knowledge, meaning mere facts, we keep the mystery at bay. There is always the chance that we grasp more than we can comprehend. If we are fortunate, we will have good teachers who will communicate their love for their subjects. It is important that we do not lose art or poetry or music in our education, for they not only open our imagination but also awaken our ability to attend and to let the subject speak for itself. Poets, musicians, artists and scientists have all sought to help us to see the great wonders in our midst. Albert Einstein is often quoted as having said, 'There are only two ways of looking at your life. One as though nothing is a miracle. The other is as though everything is a miracle.'

The poet Walt Whitman wrote:

As to me, I know of nothing else but miracles,
Whether I walk the streets of Manhattan,
Or dart my sight over the roofs of houses toward the sky,
Or wade with naked feet along the beach, just in the edge of the water,
Or stand under trees in the woods,
Or talk by day with any one I love – or sleep in the bed at night with any one I love . . .

Or watch honey-bees busy around the hive, of an August
    forenoon,
Or animals feeding in the fields,
Or birds – or the wonderfulness of insects in the air,
Or the wonderfulness of the sun-down – or of stars
    shining so quiet and bright . . .
To me, every hour of the light and dark is a miracle,
Every cubic inch of space is a miracle,
Every square yard of the surface of the earth is spread
    with the same . . .
What stranger miracles are there?[4]

Back in the seventh century, St Cuthbert declared, 'O, what wretches we are. We are so dull and full of sleep that we miss the glory that is all about us.' If only we could open our eyes.

Artists, musicians and poets, through their own media, help us to open our eyes to deeper dimensions. I believe it is also the task of the Church 'to open the eyes that are blind'. When we are fully awake, we will perceive the ordinary as extra-ordinary, and it will inspire in us wonder and awe. This is illustrated in the story of *The Little Prince*:

'The men where you live', said the little prince, 'raise five
    thousand roses in the same garden – and they do not
    find in it what they are looking for!'
'They do not find it,' I replied.
'And yet what they are looking for could be found in one
    single rose or a drop of water.'
'That is true,' I said.
And the little prince added: 'But the eyes are blind: one
    must look with the heart.'[5]

No one is fully awake or lives life to the full unless they realize they live in the presence of something greater, outside and beyond themselves. Self-consciousness often impedes us from getting beyond ourselves and prevents us from entering into the greater reality that is all around us. Wonder is at the base of true living, and wonder leads to an awareness of your kinship to the rest of creation of which you are a part and at one. In wonder we experience a mysterious union in which we become one with the subject that holds us. We no longer just behold it, we are also held by it, and not only with it but with a greater mystery that involves us both. Wonder is not just about looking; it is about our whole being. It is only when we are willing to fully give ourselves, our time and our attention, that the other will have room to give itself to us. This is true of people, of things and of the Great Other in our midst and within whom we dwell.

Wonder cannot be captured or tightly held; once we try to cling to it, it tends to disappear. It cannot be created on demand, though someone who is used to bowing before wonder can lead others to experience it for themselves. Once we begin to analyse wonder it means we have already lost it. The experience of wonder is approached with awe and is so often beyond all words. Wonder is the source of joy and it draws you out of yourself into a greater world, to the wonder of the beyond in our midst. Poets have often expressed the effects of wonder in their lives. Here is one of my favourites:

I have felt
A presence that disturbs me with the joy
Of elevated thoughts: a sense sublime
Of something far more deeply interfused,

Whose dwelling is the light of setting suns,
And the round ocean and the living air;
And the blue sky, and in the mind of man;
A emotion and a spirit, that impels
All thinking things, all objects of all thought,
And rolls through all things.[6]

Wonder often comes when we least expect it. Yet it can only reach us if we are open to it or something in life has opened up a new awareness. Sometimes a dislocation from our usual place can trigger it. It can come through the birth of a child or the death of a loved one: through something that breaks into our routine. Even those who have hardened their lives can be suddenly touched or moved by an event or a person, by a piece of music or a work of art.

Just when we are safest, there's a sunset-touch,
A fancy from a flower-bell, some one's death,
A chorus-ending from Euripides, –
And that's enough for fifty hopes and fears,
As old and new at once as nature's self,
To rap and knock and enter in our soul.[7]

## Exercise

How open are you to the mystery and wonders that come to you every day?

Aim to give yourself fully to the present moment and all that is in it. You may like to use the way of meditating on a single subject as suggested in this chapter.

Enjoy beholding and being held as part of the world.

**Prayer**

Blessed are you, Lord God Almighty,
the Creator of all that is.
Open my eyes to the wonders of creation.
Open my ears to the call of the other.
Open my heart to love all of your world.
Open my being to your glory in all things.
Blessed are you, Lord God Almighty.

#  *Love*

I was once asked to write an essay on love and found it extremely difficult. I read St Paul's description of love in his first letter to the Corinthians and realized it is easier to say what love is not than what love is. However, I remember still the conclusion I came to: 'It is better to know love and to share love than to be able to define it.' Love cannot be contained in a concept or explained, for it is part of the deep mystery of our being. We all need to know we are loved and are capable of love. Love is meant to flow into you and flow out from you; you cannot keep it to yourself. In a relationship, love is both awakened and shared. Love is the theme of many songs and films because it is so important to us:

'Love is a many-splendored thing.'
'Love is in the air.'
'Love changes everything.'
'All you need is love.'
And from the film *Love Actually*, the conclusion is that love is all around.

Possibly the best way to learn to love is by recognizing the love that is given to us. In an ideal world we are created out of love and for love. Our parents may not often express their love in words, but they demonstrate it by offering their time and attention, by giving themselves to us. Many a mother pours love into her care for the family. If she were not able to do this, the work would soon become a chore. I remember my Gran refusing to bake a cake one day saying, 'I am angry and that will spoil what I cook.'

In J. D. Salinger's *Franny and Zooey*, Franny is a 20-year-old student who has returned home from a theological college a nervous wreck. She is not eating and keeps compulsively reciting prayers. Her mother Bessie is deeply concerned for her and in loving care prepares and brings a cup of chicken soup. Franny pushes it away. This makes her brother Zooey angry and he says:

> 'I tell you one thing, Franny. One thing I know. And don't get upset. It isn't anything bad. But if it is the religious life you want, you ought to know right now that you are missing out on every single religious action that is going on in this house. You don't even have sense enough to drink when somebody brings you a cup of consecrated chicken soup – which is the only kind of chicken soup Bessie ever brings to anybody around this madhouse. So just tell me, just tell me, buddy. Even if you went out and searched the whole world for a master – some guru, some holy man, to tell you how to say your Jesus prayer properly, what good would it do you? How in hell are you going to recognize a legitimate holy man when you see one if you don't even know a cup of consecrated chicken soup when it's right in front of your nose?'[1]

Before we ever learn to love, we are loved, and it is this free gift – neither earned nor deserved – that gives strength and meaning to our whole being. It comes through our parents, from relatives and friends. This love helps us to understand the love that is there in the Originating Source of all that is.

It makes life worth living, and in return for this gift nothing is asked except that we respond to love and give love in return. Where love is poured in, let it flow out to others and infuse all you do with purpose and meaning. When life is a struggle and everything appears to be against you, remember that you are loved. When prayer seems to die and words will not come, seek to respond to love. John Chrysostom said, 'Find the door to your heart, it is the door to the kingdom of God.' In love we discover God; in love the door of our whole being is opened to a new life, a new world, and we move towards healing and wholeness.

Love is very like gravity in that it binds things together and draws things into its orbit or orbits around them. Without gravity things would fall apart or implode and fall back into nothingness. It is the same with love. Without love we are nothing. With love, healing and transformation are possible. Time and again, while visiting people who were ill or deeply troubled, I have seen a change take place due to a loving letter or, better, a visit from a loved one. One woman in hospital had a wound that would not heal. She lived alone and her only relative was a sister who she thought was not interested in her. I managed to get the sister's name and address and explain how this woman was stuck in hospital. The sister's immediate reaction was, 'Why did she not let me know?' The result was that she went to the hospital, expressed her love and concern, promised to return within a couple of days and then took her sister to stay with her family as long as was necessary. The outcome was a renewal of contact and love, and what the nursing staff described as a miraculous healing of the wound.

Love is an indescribable sense of connectedness, a common union when two move towards becoming one, which often includes an awareness of yet another, a presence, a mystery that is more than either. With this comes a feeling of well-being and belonging, affirming our worth and giving us new energy and hope. We are no longer on our own, for we are loved. We are no longer self-obsessed, for there is another in our life.

Sadly, to say 'I love you' often means 'I want to have you, possess you and own you.' A far deeper and more passionate love is about the giving of oneself to the other. This love is always respectful and gentle. The people of Spain are known to be hot-blooded people. They make a distinction between 'Te quiero', which means 'I want you', suggesting desire, need, lusting after, perhaps even control, and 'Te amo', which does not have the same undertones. Rather, it is an expression of outgoing love, of the willingness to give and to serve. This word is not used so frequently because our love is often still very self-centred. True love moves us out of our self centredness and opens up for us a whole new way of living and looking at the world. Such love is only possible when we reach out to another with our whole being. It is this sort of love, the outpouring of the self, through which God created the world: you were created for love and out of love. The very source of your being is love. In our most fragile moments we know that we are made of dust and to dust we shall return, but in the depth of our being we know there is more. We are not created out of nothing but out of love, so we will not return to nothing: our journey ends in 'lovers meeting'.

When I wonder about the world, or about life, or when I am searching for the meaning of it all, I turn to some words of Julian of Norwich, who is the first woman writer in English we know of and who lived in a time of war, plague and famine in the fourteenth century. This passage says it all:

'Would you know our Lord's meaning in this? Learn it well. Love was his meaning. Who showed it you? Love. What did he show you? Love. Why did he show you? For love. Hold fast to this, and you shall learn and know more about love, but you will never need to know or understand about anything else for ever and ever. Thus did I learn that Love was our Lord's meaning.'[2]

#  *I Am Who I Am*

**I am who I am**

I am the mystery of creation
I am the quantum expanding forth
I am the dust of creation
I am the clouds of gas becoming stars
I am the explosion creating the elements
I am the solar system set in the Milky Way
I am who I am.

I am the mystery that holds all in balance
I am the life force in all that there is
I am the common unity in the diversity
I am the waters of life on earth
I am the fire and the heat
I am the wind and the waves
I am the beginning of life on earth
I am who I am.

I am the aeons of time
I am the early life forms in the oceans
I am the first creature that moved
I am the sea creatures that swim
I am the creatures that crawl
I am the fins that became wings
I am the creatures that fly
I am all that can move
I am who I am.

I am the light and life in humans
I am the wisdom and the grace
I am the love and the joy
I am the power and the peace
I am in you and you are in me
I am who I am.

I am in all things yet beyond all things
I am what holds all things in being
I am the mystery in everything
I am the container of all
I am in you and you are in me
I am No-thing yet I fill all things
I am who I am.

 *Notes*

## Introduction

1 W. H. Gardner (ed.), *Gerard Manley Hopkins* (London: Penguin, 1963), p. 120.
2 Christopher Devlin SJ (ed.), *The Sermons and Devotional Writings of Gerard Manley Hopkins* (Oxford: Oxford University Press, 1959), p. 195 (8 December 1881, Preaching on the Immaculate Conception, by permission of Oxford University Press on behalf of the British Province of The Society of Jesus).
3 Augustine (Peter G. Walsh, Christopher Collard and Isabella Image, eds), *De Citate Dei*, Book XVI (Liverpool: Liverpool University Press, 2018).
4 St Francis of Assisi 1182–1226.

## The dangerous animal

1 Maurice Maeterlinck, *The Life of the Bee* (New York: Blue Ribbon Books, 1901).

## Wonder

1 Quoted in Michael Mayne, *Sunrise of Wonder* (London: Font, 1995), p. 109.
2 1 Corinthians 13.1–2.
3 D. H. Lawrence, 'The Egotist', in *The Complete Poems of D. H. Lawrence* (Ware: Wordsworth Editions, 1994), p. 497.
4 Walt Whitman, 'Poem of Perfect Miracle', in *Leaves of Grass* (1856).
5 Antoine de Saint-Exupéry, *The Little Prince* (London: Penguin, 1962), pp. 91–2.

6  William Wordsworth, 'Lines Composed a Few Miles above Tintern Abbey' (1798).

7  Robert Browning, *Bishop Blougram's Apology* (1855).

## Love

1  J. D. Salinger, *Franny and Zooey* (London: Penguin, 2010), pp. 127–8.

2  Richard Llewelyn (ed.), *Enfolded in Love: Daily Readings with Julian of Norwich* (London: Darton, Longman & Todd, 1980), p. 59.